ALL OF LIFE

ALL OF LIFE

A course exploring real life and real faith
inspired by *Call the Midwife*

Edited by
Bryony Taylor, David Twomey
& Rebecca Amoroso

DARTON·LONGMAN+TODD

First published as an eBook in 2020,
and in print in 2024, by
Darton, Longman and Todd Ltd
1 Spencer Court
140 – 142 Wandsworth High Street
London SW18 4JJ

Printed book ISBN: 978-0-232-53446-7
eBook ISBN: 978-0-232-53447-4

A catalogue record for this book is available from the
British Library

Designed and produced by Judy Linard
Printed and bound in Great Britain by Bell & Bain, Glasgow

CONTENTS

PREFACE
To the first printed edition

Some time has passed since Bryony, David, and Rebecca wrote and edited this book. We were on course to publish in print (alongside the eBook) in 2020, but then something happened which none of us had experienced before. We hope we never experience the like again. We won't go into too much detail about the pandemic here, but there is no doubt that this has fundamentally changed us, as individuals, as a society, and as Christians.

It is a great joy that we are once again able to meet in groups, and we are excited to share with you the wisdom and hope we have gathered in this book. One of the side effects of the pandemic was the time to watch a lot more television, and so we hope that you have seen at least a few episodes of *Call the Midwife* by now.

Much has changed since we first came together to create a discipleship course rooted in our contexts and experiences of parish life. Bryony is now a Rector in Derbyshire, David is an Airport Chaplain in Manchester, and Rebecca is a University Chaplain at Durham. But we are still committed to nurturing the discipleship of those whom we serve and continuing to grow in our own faith and ministries.

Call the Midwife continues to tell the story of the Sisters and Midwives of Nonnatus House and is entering into an era that some of us may well recognise. We have read this book again, and we are sure that the issues, essays, commentaries, and activities in this book remain as relevant – if not more relevant – today as a few years ago. While much has changed, God remains the same. Our desire to follow Christ still encourages us to love one another as we are loved. And so, we offer you this course to use in your journey, with our prayers and blessings.

Bryony, David, and Rebecca

December 2023

FOREWORD

by the

Rt Revd Dr Helen-Ann Hartley

The Rt Revd Dr Helen-Ann Hartley was previously the Chair of the Sandford St Martin Trust,[1] a non-denominational charity that advocates for excellence in religious and ethical broadcasting. She is now Bishop of Newcastle.

In 1957 the revered American journalist Edward R. Murrow – the same one whose searing broadcasts helped topple McCarthyism – referred to television as 'the opiate of the people'. He didn't mean it as a compliment. Murrow was highly critical of what he judged were television's passive audiences and the poor programmes offered them as entertainment. His remarks kicked off a debate that resonates even more loudly today. What is television for? And why do we watch so much of it?

In 2017-18, 27 million UK homes had a television and adults over the age of 16 were found to be spending on average almost 4 hours a day watching them. Given the growing popularity of streaming services like Netflix, Sky or Amazon and technology which means we can now access television through

[1] *www.sandfordawards.org.uk*

a wide variety of screens, watching whenever and wherever we want, it's no surprise that in general our relationship with television has only grown more intense and immersive.

Murrow would have been appalled – but I'd like to suggest there's a flip side to the equation.

The mass consumption of modern television arguably unites individuals and audiences across borders, community, social and educational divisions like no other mode of communication. Think of how many people around the world tuned in to watch the wedding of Prince Harry and Meghan Markle, or the hours of frenzied speculation and then bitter criticism that accompanied the final series of *Game of Thrones*, or how the shenanigans of a bunch of swimsuit-clad twenty-somethings looking for love on an island have dominated both headlines and talk around the proverbial watercooler in recent years. All that time. All that attention. So, what would happen if the power and popularity of TV could be harnessed as a force for good?

At the Sandford St Martin Trust we think that's already been happening for a long time now and that there's plenty of that sort of programming about. I mean programmes that offer a lens through which we can recognise ourselves, our neighbours, our communities and the wider world that we share. Good television can introduce us to intriguing human stories, digging deep into motivation and providing perspective and insight into what motivates people – their beliefs and moral values. This is the sort of broadcasting our Trust exists to promote and which we recognise through our annual awards: programming that engages with the world and addresses some of the big questions of what it is to be human. Quite the opposite of the sort of programming that Murrow thought was anaesthetising audiences to the world around them.

When the TV writer and dramatist Jimmy McGovern won a double Sandford St Martin Award for his much-lauded TV series *Broken* about a fictional priest (played by Sean Bean) serving his parish in a down-at-heel part of north Liverpool, he said: 'religion sounds boring to some and contentious to others. But what it is to me is a wonderful source of stories about what it is to be human and a huge part of many people's lives.'

Indeed.

At a time when regular church-attendance is in decline and it can be difficult to engage people directly in a discussion of faith or in Bible study, good TV can provide a conduit to a new and different way of engaging with God and profound questions around who we are and why we're here. For these reasons I'm very pleased to have been asked to write this foreword and to celebrate an excellent series of books. I hope they will resonate with readers and will introduce new audiences to a deeper consideration of their faith, theology, and how these are reflected in the world around them. So, hardly a source of phoney happiness, keeping us supine and passive – instead, a way to engage with the world and to explore ideas which can ultimately change the world and our understanding of it for the better.

Ultimately, I think even Edward R. Murrow would have approved of that.

INTRODUCTION
How to use this book

Many church communities are increasingly finding it difficult to engage people in small group Bible study. Most traditional Bible study courses assume a particular level of education and background. Discipleship – or 'training in the faith' – is at the heart of a healthy growing church, and yet many church leaders struggle to do this. Something that connects people regardless of their educational ability and social background is television: it's something all people can engage with easily and have something to share about. The *God on TV* book series offers the opportunity for people to explore their faith and theology through reflection on TV programmes. Television is a mirror of our society, fictional dramas enable us to put ourselves in other people's shoes, they enable us to see new perspectives. The programmes chosen for this book series tackle some contemporary moral issues that Christians need help to engage with. What does the church have to say about inclusion of gay people? What does the church have to say about disability? How do we cope with death and bereavement? These are real life issues that rarely get addressed in our discussions at church.

This book uses the long-running BBC drama *Call the Midwife* as inspiration for exploring a variety of topics about real life and real faith. Originally based on the real-life recollections of Jennifer Worth about her time working as a midwife from the 1950s in Poplar, East London, *Call the Midwife* has become one of the best-loved programmes on television. One reason for its popularity, of course, is the sense of nostalgia produced from watching scenes depicting a period of time within living memory. The programme also, because it is showing the development of a group of people who are literally dealing with 'all of life', shows us how British mores and values have changed.

All of Life is written using the principle of 'nothing about us without us' – each contributor is from the background that is being discussed. We hope that you find these materials stimulating and helpful in enabling spiritual growth in your community.

THEOLOGICAL REFLECTIONS

The first part of each chapter is one of a series of theological reflections inspired by themes raised in *Call the Midwife*. Those who have written these reflections have asked the question 'Where is God in all this?' of the themes chosen. They are provided as starting points for the group discussions that follow. Leaders may wish to read the reflection before running a session, and it may be photocopied for members of the group to read in advance if that seems appropriate.

Fr George Guiver reflects on prayer and liturgy

(the words we use in church services) from his perspective as a monk and teacher. The Revd Katie Tupling explores how attitudes to people with disabilities have and haven't changed over the years from her perspective as a priest who campaigns for inclusion of disabled people. Chine McDonald explores the experience of a previous generation of people of colour in the church and her own personal experience in the church today. The Revd Claire Jones, herself in a Civil Partnership, explores her own experiences and reflects on what has changed for LGBTQIA+ people in the church over the last half century. The Revd Frances Wilson explores the theme of vocation and how it plays out in the lives of the characters in *Call the Midwife* and what every Christian can take from their stories. Finally, the director of the Good Funeral Company, the Revd Juliet Stephenson helps us to explore that final taboo – death and dying.

COURSE MATERIALS

The second part of each chapter provides the structure and materials for a six-week study course that can be run in your community. You can choose to run the six weeks consecutively (perhaps as a discipleship course, or during Advent or Lent) or you may wish to just use one session – for example, you might want to explore how to become more inclusive for disabled people – you could simply use the session on that topic on its own. You may also wish to draw inspiration from the materials for church services. The sessions include Bible study, discussion time and a response time – recognising that people learn and engage in different ways. The sessions are completely flexible so that you can adapt them to your own context.

Although these books use the TV programmes as a springboard for discussion it is not necessary to have watched the programmes before. At the beginning of each session there is a recommended clip that can be played from the programme (many of these programmes are available on online streaming services and some on YouTube). This is not, however, essential (we recognise that not everyone has the facilities to play video in a small group setting).

Given the diverse nature of congregations, the elements of each week's session include reflective prayer activities as well as time for group discussions that make no assumptions about people's educational background and seek to meet different learning styles and spiritual preferences. Each session, if all the elements are used, should take around an hour and a half to do.

SESSION STRUCTURE

OPENING PRAYER

It is suggested that a candle is lit and the session begins with a prayer.

INTRODUCTION TO THE THEME

The theme is introduced in a paragraph to be read out to the group or in the leader's own words. You may wish to play a clip from the programme to set the scene – suggestions are made.

BIBLE READING

The Bible study part of the session involves a simple form of what is often called 'lectio divina' – 'divine reading'. It can be helpful to give group members a print-out of the Bible reading and perhaps a pen to take notes. A Bible passage is read slowly by different voices 2 or 3 times. Silence is kept for people to read along for themselves, seeing what ideas and images are standing out the most. After some time, each person is encouraged to share (without commentary) one word or phrase that stood out for them. The passage is read out again. Then each person is encouraged to share whether the same word or image stood out again or not and why. The discussion at the end of the meditation can be in the group as a whole or in pairs. This style of Bible study helps to avoid certain individuals dominating and can also be less intimidating for those not used to formal study.

QUESTIONS FOR DISCUSSION

Sometimes it can be difficult to start a conversation, especially on a sensitive topic. For the discussion part of the session we have provided a series of conversation starters. We have found the best way to run this part of the session is to photocopy the grid of questions provided, cut them out, fold and place in a bowl. Encourage group members to take a question, read it out and discuss as a group. The randomness of this can help people to open up more than if the 'leader' asks the questions directly.

Don't feel you have to try and 'answer' all the questions, the main aim is to have a fruitful and interesting discussion. Scan the questions first to see if any might be unhelpful or triggering for people in your group and exclude them. You can also leave the option to people to pass on a question if they wish.

RESPONSE TIME

Following group discussion, simple prayer response activities are suggested. Everyone learns and engages with the things of the Spirit in different ways. Where some might be stimulated by the group discussion, others may wish to respond in other ways. Each session offers some creative ideas for responding to the theme. These activities could be undertaken in a service or the output from them used in a service in church. It is not recommended to try and do all the suggested ideas in one session (it would take too long). Simply decide which activities would most work in your context or even ask your group which activity they would like to do.

CLOSING PRAYER

Some simple music is suggested that can be listened to or sung at the end of the session in addition to a formal prayer to end the session. It can be helpful to use the same beginning and ending to each session for consistency and to give group members some idea of structure.

PART 1
LITURGY AND PRAYER

THEOLOGICAL REFLECTION

by Fr George Guiver CR

Fr George Guiver is a member of the Community of the Resurrection at Mirfield and teaches liturgy.

The bright-eyed new midwife Jenny falls into the raw world of London's East End in the 1950s and is knocked for six by it. 'I never knew people lived like this.' Two completely different things make us sit up. The nuns throw themselves into the crazy hurly-burly of need, suffering and vibrant humanity with the *nous* of hard-nosed old hands, and then regularly stand back to sing beautiful offices of prayer. The contrast is sharp, but it seems to make sense. The Sisters' ability to do the job clearly comes out of their life together, centred as it is on prayer. What does this say to us?

First of all, theirs is a life together. We need each other; human beings were made for belonging together. The Sisters, like members of any community of religious sisters or brothers, are not the saints you might imagine, but the real human beings you would find in any group. Despite the problems they can have with each other and the difficulties of their daily work, a fundamental difference is made by the life they share. At its heart is prayer. We tend to think of prayer as a private, personal thing, and that is certainly part of it, but the Gospel is firstly about belonging together, including in our prayer. When I pray, I am never alone – there will always be people all over the world praying with me at the same time. We are carrying each other, and not in any old togetherness – St Paul speaks about our being one body with many organs, each contributing its part. Jesus in St John's Gospel says he is the vine and we are the branches. Christian prayer, then, is always in the Body of Christ. It's not me as an individual trying to reach out to a distant God – it is Christ in us, the Holy Spirit in our hearts, crying through our voice, 'Abba, Father'. And it is all the people all over the world, on earth and in heaven, praying with us. For the Sisters or brothers in a religious community, this is a powerful thing. God makes himself known in our togetherness as we pray. Scattered around the district doing their tough duties and working to keep Nonnatus House running, the sisters depend on the times they drop everything and pray together. What can we do to discover this kind of prayer? We shall see shortly.

The next thing to say about the prayer of the nuns is that it carries them – as Sister Monica Joan says, 'We need not choose our thoughts, the words are aligned, like a rope for us to cling to.' You can rest your busy head, with all its thoughts, problems, excitements, worries, and allow yourself to float like a boat on this river of God's Word. You may notice that the nuns' services consist almost entirely of words from Scripture, nearly all of it taken from the Psalms. These extraordinary texts don't do what you would normally expect from prayers. They are packed with daily life – there is nothing else like them in the Bible and perhaps in the whole of ancient literature. They help us bring before God all the stuff going on around us, but also deep down inside. We don't need to think about what to say, we let these words speak to us, and speak for us to God. These services have been well tried and tested over many centuries, and if you pray them as the nuns do, they become a sort of living-room, ready-furnished, that we walk into from the hurly-burly of life. From this we learn that Christian prayer is partly a way that is given, handed on, and we can simply pick it up in trust and get on with it, knowing that here is wisdom.

When Jenny, who is not a churchgoer, wanders into the Sisters' Chapel, drawn by their singing, we are not sure what is going through her mind, but we can see this is an encounter for her, something powerful. This is how all Christian worship ought to be. On the other hand, in that same service, probably not all the Sisters will be feeling anything very powerful, perhaps not feeling much at all. That's okay – it's what happens over the long term that counts. Today when we go to a service in church we expect to have a good experience. Why? Is life in the family always like a scene from *Gone with the Wind*? Is our family life or our work all good experiences? No – good experiences come and go, but a lot of life in the home is sheer ordinariness, with lots of routine. That is life, and that is prayer, and all the time deeper things are going on underneath. The true value lies in sticking with it – the family, our job, our prayer. Get on with it. So, in various places in the New Testament we are told to 'persevere in prayer'. There is something here about Christian maturity.

In one scene Jenny wanders at night through an alley in a red-light district, with sex workers about their business on the pavement or behind the windows. Incongruously, the background music is of the nuns singing a psalm in their Chapel. The contrast might seem grotesque, but these two things in fact belong perfectly together, and this is the gospel. Christ came among us, and above all for people like those in the alley; God entered into all of life, no holds barred. There is nothing prim or prudish about the Sisters in their Chapel. They know it all belongs together. Many people today struggle to pray, and one thing that can help us is to look outwards, to take serious account of the state of the world we are in, and to take a particular interest in all the people who are struggling: the gospel draws attention to the poor, the sick, the heavy-laden. And, yes, the sinners, which we all are. The gospel asks us to recognise our own affinity with the sex-workers in the alley. As we see the state our world is in, we can't but think that it needs a Christianity that is strong, to help bring sanity to it. And Christianity will only be that if it is strong in God, and that means prayer. So scenes like the alley, or TV news of people suffering and under bombardment, boatloads of refugees trying to escape hell, or all the unhappinesses of our home country, ought to be a clarion-call to roll up our sleeves like Sister Evangelina, and energetically embrace God's summons to pray as one people.

Jesus talked about us finding life abundant, living life to the full. Today we often talk about fulfilment or human flourishing in a way that Jesus didn't mean. They are not the same. Fulfilment in particular is a dangerous term, reflecting as it does our preoccupation today with ourselves and getting what we want. Some may remember the film *The African Queen*, about a boat in which Humphrey Bogart and Katharine Hepburn brave rapids, monsoons, leeches, crocodiles, German gunboats, bombs and, in the end drag themselves ashore through thick mud in pouring rain, triumphant. Words like flourishing or fulfilment seem a bit limp here: dragging themselves through the mud Hepburn and Bogart know they have *LIVED*. St Irenaeus famously said, 'the glory of God is a human being fully alive'. In Poplar, Jenny had to deal with some of the worst life can throw at anyone, but she gives thanks that she has *lived*. Praying our daily prayers and also doing our bit for the betterment of the world are more than mere pious duty. They are essential sources of living life to the full.

Having been driven to pray by the state of the world, what, then, do we do? Where do we start? The Sisters are Anglican, and what we hear them singing are words of the *Book of Common Prayer*. The Prayer Book used to be a staple of people's prayer, praying the Collects, different parts of Morning and Evening prayer, and reading the Scriptures. Here there was material for them to use that went back thousands of years and was relevant as ever. When people prayed these prayers, they will have had a sense of praying the prayers of the Church, and will have trusted these prayers as sources of Christian wisdom. That tradition has been widely lost, and people feel the lack. And so many people are turning to modern forms of daily prayer that come out of that tradition. There is a good choice available in bookshops, and also now an abundance of apps to pray with a tablet or phone (see the list at the end of this chapter). We are in a time of exploring, and it is to be hoped that we can settle down to forms of prayer that we know other Christians are using too, aware that we are together in a common exercise.

In finding where to start, let's look at the nuns again. Firstly, they are aware of being with the great Body of Christ. Christ is among them, and in them, and around them in all the people on earth and in heaven who are praying at the same time. Furthermore, they drop everything and come together. It is good to seek every opportunity to join with others in offering the daily prayers – it might be in church, with our neighbours, or going to pray the community's prayers with somebody in hospital. The key is that it is a *form* of prayer that is used by the Church, not just me on my own.

This tradition of which I have been speaking makes major use of the Scriptures. The sisters start with verses from Scripture, they pray the Psalms; then they will listen to a reading, followed in the main services by a Canticle from the new Testament, and ending with prayers which include the Lord's Prayer. It is often said that water is magical stuff – there's nothing so special in it to look at, hardly any taste or smell, and no colour, but it does amazing things. The Scriptures are similar – they work away in the depths of our souls transforming our hidden parts. This kind of prayer is a stream of Scripture. One of the nice things about swimming in the sea is that you can close your eyes and let it gently pull you about.

Talk about the body brings us back to our humanity. We are full human beings, and we live life with the whole of ourselves, not just in our heads. The nuns, for instance, sing when they pray. People don't sing today, and as the gospel is about being whole human beings, it is part of the Church's mission to get people singing. There is no reason why we shouldn't sing, even when alone. There is a need to recover this lost part of our humanity which can be a huge help to praying. Try just singing a hymn for your prayers. Then again, we live with our eyes. We are looking and responding all day long, and this can be another great help to prayer – for instance by using a picture or an icon or going into church to pray.

Another part of the Sisters' prayer which we don't see in the TV series is their private prayer. In religious communities everyone is committed to praying quietly each day, bringing our own personal prayers, or simply sitting quietly, all ears and eyes for

God. A good way of doing this is again by drawing on the Scriptures. Reading a short passage from the Gospels will always provide a take-off point for reflective prayer. Such quiet prayer is not easy for everybody, but it nearly always comes as a gift for those who are already praying the daily prayers of the Church. Out of the flow of holy words comes an ability to be quiet. We often make the mistake of trying to start with the personal prayer, rather than with the Body of Christ.

How often do we need to pray? A long-standing tradition is for Christians to pray in the morning and evening. In religious communities it can be more. Those tough Sisters of Nonnatus House, in common with most Anglican sisterhoods of the nineteenth and early twentieth centuries, will have prayed seven services a day, most of them short, and we are told in episode 2 that they started at 4.30 in the morning! They will also have had a Eucharist every day, and time for their quiet prayer. It sounds mad, but for those attracted to it and who love it, it works. In my own community we have four services a day, plus Eucharist and quiet prayer, but we used to do the full seven, even when doing very tough work in South Africa, helping Black people to gain an education, and joining in the struggle against Apartheid. This might illustrate the fact that prayer always demands commitment and a degree of Christian maturity. In the circumstances of modern life, many people would find it difficult to sit down, alone or with others, and pray a set form of prayer that takes, say, 15 minutes to do. But if you can only do it in the morning, there is nothing to stop you saying a quick 'Our Father' or other prayer in the evening, either in tranquillity, or waiting for the bus, or doing the washing up. The *doing* is the key, not the feeling.

For Christians there is ultimately no such thing as private prayer. Jesus taught us to say, 'Our Father', not 'My Father'. There is a natural consequence: we need a sure anchor, which is public worship, 'going to church'. The whole emphasis of the New Testament is that we belong together. For instance:

> *Once you were not a people, but now you are God's people.* (1 Peter 2)

> *[Make] every effort to maintain the unity of the Spirit in the bond of peace. There is one body and one Spirit, just as you were called to the one hope of your calling, one Lord, one faith, one baptism, one God and Father of all, who is above all and through all and in all.* (Ephesians 4:1-6)

There are both human and supernatural reasons for this. If you belong to a club, irregular attendance will leave you out of touch. Similarly, being a Christian is a skill like playing the piano or football. Pianists and footballers need to practise in a regular pattern or they will lose their skill. Keep up-and-running or you will go cold. If we have a strong relationship with someone, we need to be in touch regularly, and for Christians that 'someone' is the Lord in his Body the Church. The local branch of it is our congregation. It's not just about meeting *my* needs – the others there need me too, and my contribution, and when I fail to get to church I am letting the others down. More might depend on you than you realize. We also need to be taken out of ourselves – our private prayers and thoughts and views on things always need to be widened – the bigger the horizon, the more we are likely to get towards the truth. Over and above all that, there is something in Christian worship that comes to us in no other way: God does things for us in public worship that we only find there. Worshipping together is part of the Christian package, and without it we only get a shadow of what is on offer.

This worship needs to connect with our daily life in many ways, including our rhythmic experience of that unique thing, the week. So, the main acts of worship are weekly, and if possible on Sunday, the day on which the Lord arose from the dead. At the heart of Christian worship stands the Lord's Supper on the Lord's Day. We take bread and wine and give thanks over them and share them, and in doing that we are put in living touch with the cross and the resurrection. This is made clear in a wonderful prayer said at the heart of the service. It begins with 'Lift up your hearts', and goes on through the 'Holy, Holy, Holy' and the story of the Last Supper, and then carries us into the great mystery of our redemption through the cross and resurrection. It draws us onto God's escalator, so that we join, as it were, the angels on Jacob's ladder, and end by giving our resounding '*Amen*'.

This prayer is very Jewish, and a similar prayer is still used in the synagogue today with food and a cup of wine. When the Gospels say that Jesus took the bread and wine and 'gave thanks', they are referring to him saying (singing) what is in essence this very prayer, and Christians have continued to do it over 2000 years, passing it on Sunday by Sunday. Isn't that amazing and exciting? Worship is bigger than us, and there is a lot in it we need to study in order to understand it for what it is. Why is it so important? One clue is found in the word 'Communion'. Christianity is not about being a club of like-minded activists, but one body at unity with itself and the Lord who is the source of its life, all of us in communion. The Christian life of prayer is an ongoing journey through which over the years we grow. I can't just do praying on my own. In order to do it, I need to go regularly to the Christian takeaway and come away resourced for my own prayers.

So, if you want life, you could do worse than think of Nonnatus House.

RECOMMENDED PRAYER AIDS
APPS AND WEBSITES

PrayerMate App – manage prayer lists and get daily encouragement to pray https://www.prayermate. net/

Ignatian Spirituality – includes daily meditations, podcasts and apps https://www.ignatianspirituality. com/

Pray As You Go – daily guided prayer online or as a podcast https://pray-as-you-go.org/

Daily Prayer App from the Church of England
https://www.churchofengland.org/apps

The Daily Disconnect – daily prayer podcast from the Carmelite Order http://www.carmelites.net/daily-disconnect-podcast/

COURSE MATERIALS
by Fr David Twomey

When we use the word 'Liturgy', we often mean a public service with a set form of words. In the life of the Church of England, it most clearly relates to the forms of prayer for the Eucharist, as well as Morning and Evening Prayer. However, we don't tend to use the word 'Liturgy' much. We might talk about attending worship or going to a service instead.

However, this doesn't quite get to the heart of it. After all, Liturgy isn't just the words we use, although they are important. Liturgy is an action, the 'work of the people' to translate the Greek. It is a gathering together with God's people so that we might encounter him. That gathering and encountering does something; it marks us out as being God's people and builds our relationships, both with each other and with the God we seek to serve.

This session seeks to explore our experience of Liturgy and how we encounter God within it. It also encourages us to reflect on the place of Liturgy in our own discipleship.

OPENING PRAYER

A candle is lit and these words are said:

'This candle is to remind us of God's presence with us.'

Silence is kept.

OPTIONAL: WATCH CALL THE MIDWIFE *Series 1, episode 3 (49:19-55:30): Jenny goes to meet a patient as the Sisters sing Compline.*

Series 4, episode 2 (50:09- 55:30): Revd Tom Hereward creates a simple liturgy for a family grieving a stillborn baby.

INTRODUCTION

Group leaders may wish to read this out loud or introduce the theme in their own words.

Call the Midwife shows the Sisters of St Raymond Nonnatus at prayer, both privately and as a community. The Liturgy lies at the very heart of their life and work. The rhythm of prayer is the heartbeat of all that takes place, both in Nonnatus and in the show generally.

Indeed, for the Sisters it is the catalyst for their ministry. It helps them to *be*, so that they might go and *do*. In a way, this is also true for the nurses who share their lives. Some of those who live at Nonnatus are at the very fringes of faith but they find a community of welcome, which offers room to grow and air to breathe. For some, that experience is life changing and opens the door to faith and vocation. This is certainly true for Cynthia, who starts out as a midwife then goes on to join the Order.

The sights and sounds of the Sisters at prayer provide moment of connection; for example, in the Christmas Special of 2012, Sister Evangelina and nurse Jenny Lee are shown giving an elderly, rootless lady called Mrs Jenkins a bath as the Sisters sing the Advent Hymn 'O Come, O come Emmanuel'. This powerfully invites us to reflect that the Christ-child took human flesh and so the human world, the human body, bears the Divine Image. Our minds are drawn to Matthew 25 and the powerful truth that Christ is present in those people and places where we least expect to find him.

On occasions, those same sights and sounds offer a moment of contrast; we hear Psalm 51 as Jenny looks around a red-light district. The words of the Psalm, which appeal to the mercy of God amidst our human frailty, seem far from the images we see on the screen.

For us too, Liturgy can offer us Community, Connections, and Contrasts. We gather with others, often who have different experiences and backgrounds to our own, but we are united in our common striving to know the Lord. We hear the words of Scripture and receive Christ, either spiritually or in the Eucharist. Sometimes, in the midst of busy lives and a noisy world, we hear that invitation to discover different ways of being and doing.

LECTIO DIVINA

Listen carefully as someone reads this passage from the Bible, then take some time afterwards to reflect in silence on what you have just heard.

The passage is provided in one translation here, you may wish to use a different version (visit Biblegateway.com to find alternative versions).

Sometimes it is helpful to provide group members with a copy so that they can read along.

ACTS 2:42-47 [NRSV]

They devoted themselves to the apostles' teaching and fellowship, to the breaking of bread and the prayers. Awe came upon everyone, because many wonders and signs were being done by the apostles. All who believed were together and had all things in common; they would sell their possessions and goods and distribute the proceeds to all, as any had need. Day by day, as they spent much time together in the temple, they broke bread at home and ate their food with glad and generous hearts, praising God and having the goodwill of all the people. And day by day the Lord added to their number those who were being saved.

℘

- Listen again to the verses, read in a different voice.
- Is there a word, or a sentence, that jumps out at you? Which of these words are for you today? Why?
- Either in pairs or in the main group, share with each other the word or phrase that stood out.
- Read through once more with a different reader. Has that word or phrase changed?

NOTES FOR LEADERS

- Note the fourfold character of the early Church gatherings:

  Teaching   Fellowship   Eucharist   Prayer

- How are these still found in Church life and discipleship today?
- For the earliest Christians, their experience of Liturgy gave shape to their lives. The generosity of the God they experienced in Word and Sacrament inspired them to offer a generosity of their own, both within the family of the Church and outside it too. Their joy drew others into that worshipping community.

  How might our worship do likewise today?

DISCUSSION TOPICS

Sometimes it can be difficult to start a conversation, especially on a sensitive topic. For the discussion part of the session we have provided a series of conversation starters. We have found the best way to run this part of the session is to photocopy the grid of questions, cut them out, fold and place in a bowl. Encourage group members to take a question, read it out and discuss as a group. The randomness of this can help people to open up more than if the 'leader' asks the questions directly.

Don't feel you have to try and 'answer' all the questions, the main aim is to have a fruitful and interesting discussion. Scan the questions first to see if any might be unhelpful or triggering for people in your group and exclude them. You can also leave the option to people to pass on a question if they wish.

You may wish also to write some discussion questions of your own on this theme that will suit your context. Ideally, this section of the session should feel relaxed and informal.

'The liturgy is of comfort to the disarrayed mind. We need not choose our thoughts; the words are aligned, like a rope for us to cling to.' - Sister Monica Joan

Have you ever had that experience of a 'scattered mind'?

How did the liturgy connect (or not) with you then?

Which do you find happens most often for you in worship:

Community?
Connections?
Contrasts?

How can worship be a springboard for the mission of the Church today?

Have you ever had an experience where you really felt close to God in worship?

If you feel comfortable, can you share with the group what made that experience so significant.

What questions do you have about what we do in Church?

What parts of the Liturgy really speak to you?

Are there any parts you find unhelpful?

The early Christians dedicated themselves to teaching, fellowship, the Eucharist and prayer.

Which of these is most important for you?

Where do you find it easiest to pray? At home? In Church?

In the natural world?

How do you think someone who has never encountered Christian worship before might feel in your Church?

How would you teach someone to pray?

RESPONSE TIME

Below are some suggestions for activities to respond to the Bible reading and group discussion. You may wish to use one or a few of these suggestions or come up with an idea of your own. Appropriate music could be played to encourage a prayerful atmosphere. You may wish to begin and end with a time of silence.

1. End your session with a short service of Midday Prayer or Compline:
   Examples for each day can be found here, both in contemporary and traditional language:
   https://www.churchofengland.org/prayer-and-worship/join-us-daily-prayer

2. Make a 'Rope Prayer'
   Write on a piece of card a favourite word, phrase or prayer from the Liturgy.
   This might be from the Eucharist, Daily Prayer, a sentence of Scripture or from another source. They might also have been prayers which have really spoken to us in hard times.
   Attach the prayers to a piece of rope or string. These can be a reminder of Sister Monica Joan's phrase about the Liturgy being a 'rope for us to cling to'.

3. Use famous prayers as a guided meditation.
   The leader slowly offers some familiar prayers, leaving a long pause (1 minute minimum) in between each line of the prayer to allow people to reflect on the words.

Examples to use could be:
The Lord's Prayer
The Prayer of Preparation (Almighty God, to whom all hearts be open…)
The Second Collect for Evening Prayer (Lighten our darkness, we beseech thee…)

4. Listen to some examples of monastic chant.
    Hold a time of silence afterwards. How has God spoken to you?

5. Work as a team to plan a simple Liturgy for a particular group of people: e.g. *children and families, those with English as an additional language, those with dementia, etc.*
    What are the important things that will guide your decision making?
    How will you make it appropriate to that group?

You may wish to close the response time by singing this chant or another suitable song:

> *O Lord, hear my prayer,*
> *O Lord, hear my prayer,*
> *When I call, answer me.*
> *O Lord, hear my prayer,*
> *O Lord, hear my prayer,*
> *Come and listen to me.*

(Taizé Community)

This session may have touched on some difficult, and personal themes.

Invite a time of stillness so that people can think about something that they have found challenging or an action they need to undertake in response to this session.

FINAL PRAYER

Spend some time in silent prayer praying for the person to your right. Then read this prayer in conclusion:

Visit this place, O Lord, we pray,
and drive far from it the snares of the enemy;
may your holy angels dwell with us and guard
   us in peace,
and may your blessing be always upon us;
through Jesus Christ our Lord.
Amen.

PART 2

DISABILITY/ ABILITY

THEOLOGICAL REFLECTION

by the Revd Katie Tupling

The Revd Katie Tupling is a priest in the Church of England who campaigns for full inclusion of disabled people in the church.

We have come a long way in understanding disabilities since the time when *Call the Midwife* was set – we no longer automatically send newly-diagnosed disabled children to residential homes, nor remove babies from the arms of disabled parents and enforce adoption. Disabled people now have a greater presence in the workforce and have better access to the norms of wider society. The Disability Discrimination Act (1995) and the subsequent Equalities Act (2010) have challenged attitudes and access, giving more robust guidelines to workplaces, businesses and public buildings around the challenges faced by disabled people.

However, in a recent poll on social media, disabled people and able-bodied allies were asked about the issues and challenges facing disabled people today. The anecdotes revealed that so many of the attitudes dealt with in *Call the Midwife* are still prevalent in wider society, and in the assumptions people are projecting onto disabled people. Issues highlighted included: a hostile environment (through politics and media outlets) where disabled people are portrayed as benefit cheats; a lack of understanding about the actual capabilities of disabled people; reactions of pity or disdain when people meet disabled people; assumptions around workplace, love and parenting capabilities; and the simple issues of physically accessing most buildings, which are designed for people on two functioning legs with fully functioning eyesight and good hearing.

Many disabled people today are seeking to celebrate what a long-term condition might mean, how disability can enhance their personal growth and understanding of what it means to be human. Three particular episodes of *Call the Midwife* highlight some of these issues.

DISABILITY CHALLENGES WHAT WE THINK IS ACCEPTABLE

In Series 5, episode 1 a couple with two mature children are heading off to the maternity home as baby number 3, something of an afterthought by their own admission, appears to be on the way. Their conversation revolves around the family mantra, 'let's focus on what we have got rather than what we haven't got'. The context is poverty and wealth, and now the challenge of feeding a family of five rather than a family of four.

The baby, a little girl, is successfully delivered and living, but the shock for the midwife is that all four of the baby's limbs have severely restricted growth, and the doctor fears there will be significant malformations to the internal organs too. In a conversation later with one of the nuns, the midwife uses the word 'ghastly' of the baby. The nurse caring for the mother overnight delays introducing her to her new daughter, using a variety of excuses, so the mother doesn't see her baby straight away. The advice given by higher medical professionals is to allow the baby to slip away quietly in the night by withdrawing food and water, an outcome which is deemed better for the family and for the child itself. However, the storyline unfolds with the baby crying for food and the soft-hearted doctor feeding her milk from a bottle and cuddling her through the night. The baby girl survives and, in the doctor's own words, appears to want to live. However, on first meeting his daughter and the revelation that she's not what he would class as a normal baby, the father's emotional response to the doctor is the question, 'how could you let *that* live?' By contrast, the mother takes her baby girl in her arms, and – on looking at her limbs – she says, 'What a mess, but we'll sort something out, because you're mine.'

Many people born with disabilities grow up with the narrative around them that they are not normal, and therefore not fully acceptable. Missing or damaged limbs can bring about a reaction of pity from others in society. Quite often what we have had spoken over us as children is the phrase, 'Oh, what a shame'. Sometimes it is embedded in the disappointment that we may not achieve or have access to everything that an able-bodied society offers. There is usually an undercurrent of pity that we are not fully formed human beings, and we therefore challenge what it means to be human.

How does a parent with a living Christian faith, holding in their arms a baby born with physical difference, read the words of Psalm 139 which says, 'I praise you, for I am fearfully and wonderfully made'? Disability challenges the assumption that to be perfectly made by a loving God, means to have every part of us working fully.

In *Call the Midwife*, baby Susan unites the whole family at the end of the episode around their own philosophy that you 'work with what you have not what you haven't'. The family know that they will have to face the stares and pity of all around them but belonging to family is more important than society's expectations.

DISABILITY CHALLENGES OUR SENSE OF SELF-WORTH AND WIDER VALUE

Series 7, episode 3 brings disability much closer to home, when we meet Mrs Lunt and her daughter. Mrs Lunt and her husband are expecting their third child, but it becomes apparent by the way she moves and speaks that something is wrong with Mrs Lunt, and midwives draw in the doctor to discern a diagnosis. After being sent for neurological tests, it turns out Mrs Lunt has Huntington's disease, and after some investigation her daughter Wendy is found to have the juvenile version of the same condition. The obvious physical struggles that Mrs

Lunt and her daughter have with their bodies, is set against the parallel storyline of a local beauty pageant. It is interesting to see the difference between the importance of a so-called perfect body, and the lack of function of an increasingly disabled body. Against the compère's announcement at the start of the contest, 'prepare to be dazzled by perfection', comes a family who are struggling to stay together in the light of compromised health and an uncertain future.

Mrs Lunt's imperfect body results in an inability to change her new baby's nappy, which raises questions over her competency. There is no discussion around ongoing home support to enable her to be a mother for as long as possible – removal and adoption is the given. Wendy's compromised body means she will have to go and live in a residential home for children with severe disabilities. Mr Lunt is left questioning his viability as a husband and a father in the light of disability and the depleted household.

DISABILITY CHALLENGES OUR ASSUMPTIONS AROUND RELATIONSHIPS AND HUMAN CAPACITY

Love is a tricky concept to explain; felt deeply, but hard to put into words. We know when we love someone, and how we feel about them, but to an outsider it may make no sense. We see in society a changing understanding of what love can mean between two people. Much of our understanding moves beyond the inherited binary of male and female, and we understand love in a broader sense. However, disabled people still find themselves on the receiving end of the assumption that we are somehow less than able to love another person.

This is played out in a very obvious way in current American politics. If a disabled person marries another person, their welfare benefits are immediately cut. So many disabled people live with their long-term partners and simply cannot afford to risk getting married. It seems like there is a tax on disabled love. Many disabled people on social media report surprise when it is discovered that they are in long-term partnerships, or even married. 'How lovely that someone would marry you!' is often said to a disabled person. It is as though the able-bodied person showing love is making a huge sacrifice and lowering themselves to a place of lifelong partnership with someone who cannot give them the same love in return.

In Series 3, episode 5 of *Call the Midwife,* we meet Sally and Jacob. Both are in a residential home for disabled adults: Sally has Down's syndrome, and Jacob has cerebral palsy. It is assumed that none of the residents are in anything other than platonic friendships and are not capable of anything more. As the episode unfolds we discover that Sally is pregnant by Jacob. Although Sally is a 30-year old woman, due to her Down's syndrome she is assumed to have the intellectual capacity of a child, and therefore the doctor overseeing her care presumes that she has been raped, rather than giving consent. Indeed, as another character observed, 'it is an offence to have intercourse with a mental defective'.

Sally is taken back to her parents' house: they are furious and threatening legal action against whoever has 'molested' their daughter. Meanwhile Jacob overhears that Sally is pregnant and goes across town on the bus to find her. Sally and Jacob reveal to the midwives and Sally's mother that they are in fact boyfriend and girlfriend and very much in love. Jacob informs them that he intends to marry Sally and make things right. Sally's mother is incredulous and goes to strike Jacob for being impertinent.

In an emotional moment, Jacob says to Sally's mother, 'There is a part of me that you cannot see, but she can. And if I know she is loved then I can go on living'.

Sally's baby is premature and is stillborn. Sally returns to the residential home with the blessing of her mother and father and discovers that Jacob has been forcibly moved to a residential home in Scotland. He is told that he has family there, and his reply rather sadly is, 'I wouldn't know'. The closing scene has Sally sitting on her bed glad to be 'home', where she feels truly herself and normal, and holding a note that says, 'love from Jacob'.

We have come a long way since the time that *Call the Midwife* was set, and yet the struggles still seem to be very real in society. In this episode the young Curate desperately wishes to fight the corner of Jacob and the injustice that Jacob is being labelled as incapable of his own thoughts and genuine love. The manager of the Residential Home voices an opinion that one day these attitudes will change, but for the moment they must both work with what they have.

In today's society we see the same questions over who can and should love. The boundaries are very clear when it's about adults and children but are less clear when it is between adults who have disabilities. Many disabled adults are still treated as children; and, therefore, the rights given to 'normal' adults are stripped away from many disabled adults. It could be argued that what makes us fully and truly human is our capacity to love and be loved. Jacob and Sally in *Call the Midwife* are both legal adults but deemed incapable of love because of their disability.

From a Christian point of view it is difficult to hold this line of thought in relation to God who loves us first. If a human being is deemed incapable of loving another human, are they therefore equally incapable of loving or being loved by God?

Equally, the storyline in *Call the Midwife* raises the question of parenting. Although the episode never deals with this as a reality, as Sally's baby is stillborn, what would have happened had the baby lived? At that time disabled people were considered incapable of caring for and loving babies. The child would have been taken from them and given up for adoption automatically. Thankfully today we have many systems in place that begin with the assumption that a disabled person can be a parent and asks what support might be needed in order for both to flourish, and when the system works well everybody benefits.

CLOSING THOUGHTS

Disability, in the time of *Call the Midwife*, was a problem to be solved rather than an opportunity to learn. Segregation rather than integration, lack of capacity rather than the ability to teach others, a drain rather than a blessing.

Today, society is better at valuing all that disabled people have to offer. It is better at making the changes needed to enable disabled people to belong and flourish. It is better at recognising and celebrating the many gifts and skills which disabled people have – and the ingenuity shown by disabled people who often have to improvise and adapt.

We have come a long way – and the journey is not over yet.

COURSE MATERIALS
by Fr David Twomey

One of the underlying themes of *Call the Midwife* is its approach to issues of disability. There are a number of individuals who encounter the experience of disability in the series. Some respond with fear or anger; others do so with love and compassion. Often there is a sense of movement from the one to the other.

This session seeks to explore how some of the attitudes and perceptions surrounding issues of ability/disability have changed over time. It also seeks to explore our own experiences of those issues, as well as our personal responses to those who differ from us, both within and outside of the Church.

OPENING PRAYER

A candle is lit and these words are said:

'This candle is to remind us of God's presence with us.'

Silence is kept.

OPTIONAL: WATCH CALL THE MIDWIFE
Series 2, episode 4 (21:43-22:53): The Sisters discuss

the case of a child with spina bifida (49:20-50:32). This shows the parents trying to decide whether to place the baby into St Gideon's.

Series 5, episode 1 (27:09- 32:23): Rhoda and Susan Mullucks

INTRODUCTION
Group leaders may wish to read this out loud or introduce the theme in their own words.

Throughout the series, the Sisters and staff at Nonnatus House regularly accompany those parents who face a sense of pain, of loss, of things appearing to have gone wrong. They are with people in the most hurtful and painful experiences of life. The Sisters listen, pray, offer practical help and encourage families to go on.

There is also a spotlight, a challenging spotlight, placed on the attitudes of the time; parents and their children regularly meet with disgust from other members of the community, endure patronising encounters with medical professionals, and experience pressure to send their children to institutions. A profound example of this is demonstrated in the escalation of the thalidomide crisis. The seemingly cold, clinical response of many professionals at the time is unflinchingly shown; for example, a doctor refers to baby Ruby Cottingham as an 'it' and, indeed, Ruby is subsequently left to die by the Ward Sister as she believes it to be kinder. By contrast, Sister Julienne holds the dying Ruby and speaks the words of Isaiah 43. There is in this a modelling of compassion and a rebuking of cruelty, which springs from a belief that all are made in the image and likeness of God.

This love lived out makes a difference to those who encounter it. Rhoda Mullucks is a parent whose daughter Susan is affected by Thalidomide, and who comes to accept and love her daughter and fights for her flourishing at every step.

Perhaps the greatest gift that *Call the Midwife* offers is that it shows us those living with disabilities and living well, fully part of their family and community. Characters such as Susan Mullucks are cared for by dedicated parents and siblings. The Sisters of Nonnatus House show, in many cases, how the initial experience of shock or trauma can be redeemed by love, albeit with the recognition that life will not be as they envisaged.

There is a gift given, a life to be treasured and valued.

LECTIO DIVINA

Listen carefully as someone reads this passage from the Bible, then take some time afterwards to reflect in silence on what you have just heard.

The passage is provided in one translation here, you may wish to use a different version (visit Biblegateway.com to find alternative versions). Sometimes it is helpful to provide group members with a copy so that they can read along.

JOHN 9:1-5 [NRSV]

As he walked along, Jesus saw a man blind from birth. His disciples asked him, 'Rabbi, who sinned, this man or his parents, that he was born blind?' Jesus answered, 'Neither this man nor his parents sinned; he was born blind so that God's works might be revealed in him. We must work the works of him who sent me while it is day; night is coming when no one can work. As long as I am in the world, I am the light of the world.'

ω

- Listen again to the verses, read in a different voice.
- Is there a word, or a sentence, that jumps out at you? Which of these words are for you today? Why?
- Either in pairs or in the main group, share with each other the word or phrase that stood out.

Read through once more with a different reader. Has that word or phrase changed?

NOTES FOR LEADERS

- Jesus rejects the prevailing assumption linking sin to disability. He affirms that God is working through each of us. This would have been a hugely radical statement to make in that time.
- It is the man healed who realises that Jesus is the Son of God: 'Never since the world began has it been heard that anyone opened the eyes of a person born blind. If this man were not from God, he could do nothing.'
- The Pharisees later reject the interpretation of the man born blind saying: 'You were born in sin and you would teach us?' How ready are we to learn from those different to us?

DISCUSSION TOPICS

Sometimes it can be difficult to start a conversation, especially on a sensitive topic. For the discussion part of the session we have provided a series of conversation starters. We have found the best way to run this part of the session is to photocopy the grid of questions, cut them out, fold and place in a bowl. Encourage group members to take a question, read it out and discuss as a group. The randomness of this can help people to open up more than if the 'leader' asks the questions directly.

Don't feel you have to try and 'answer' all the questions, the main aim is to have a fruitful and interesting discussion. Scan the questions first to see if any might be unhelpful or triggering for people in your group and exclude them. You can also leave the option to people to pass on a question if they wish.

You may wish also to write some discussion questions of your own on this theme that will suit your context. Ideally, this section of the session should feel relaxed and informal.

'He was born so that God's works might be revealed in him.'

How might we be called to reveal God's works?

Where can you see changes in our attitudes towards disabled people?

Do you think that people suffer from or live with disabilities?

How are those phrases different?

Do you agree that there is still social stigma attached to mental health?

How might that stigma show itself?

Have you ever encountered anyone with disabilities?

How did you feel about it?

Did anything surprise you?

Are those with disabilities 'Superhuman' or simply human?

Do you think that people still believe that disability and sin are linked somehow?

How might you challenge it?

In Series 2 of *Call the Midwife* a mother gives birth to a child with spina bifida. At the beginning, she can't look at her baby.

How might she have been feeling?

"'Life is never without hope.'"
Sister Julienne

Do you think that's true?

"'Sometimes in life you've got to be grateful for what you have got, not what you've not got.'"
– Rhoda Mullucks

Do you agree? Are there times when you have found this to be true?

In Series 3 we meet Sally and Jacob, two young people with disabilities who have a child together. The relationship is consensual, but Jacob is removed from St Gideon's.

How might the desire to protect people stop them from flourishing?

RESPONSE TIME

Below are some suggestions for activities to respond to the Bible reading and group discussion. You may wish to use one or a few of these suggestions or come up with an idea of your own. Appropriate music could be played to encourage a prayerful atmosphere. You may wish to begin and end with a time of silence.

1. Make a collage or an ikon of Jesus' encounter with the blind man in John 9.

2. Learn the words to the Lord's Prayer in Makaton:
    https://www.youtube.com/
    watch?v=eEt9ihvsekU
    Could you use this in worship?

3. Hold a Prayer Walk around your Church building or your local community.

    *   Where are the physical or emotional barriers? How might they prevent people getting involved in Church or parish life?
    *   Pray for those who might be affected. Pray for those with the responsibility of making change happen.
    *   *(Bear in mind that not every disability is visible or physical in nature.)*

4. Write an acrostic poem using one of the following phrases:

    *   Fullness of life

- Wholeness
- The Glory of God

5. Read through Mark 5:1-20, which depicts a
    man isolated from his community because he
    is 'possessed'. We might say that he has mental
    health/self-harm issues.

    - Take it in turns to read the passage slowly,
      whilst quietly singing or listening to the
      hymn 'Just as I am, without one plea'.
    - *You could also use 1 Samuel 16:14-23
      (David and Saul) combined with music on
      the harp.*

You may wish to close the response time by singing
this chant or another suitable song:

> *Take, O take me as I am.
> Summon out what I shall be.
> Set your seal upon my heart
> And live in me.*
>
> *(Iona Community)*

This session may have touched on some difficult,
and personal themes.

Invite a time of stillness so that people can think
about something that they have found challenging
or an action they need to undertake in response to
this session.

FINAL PRAYER

Spend some time in silent prayer praying for the person to your right. Then read this prayer in conclusion:

Visit this place, O Lord, we pray,
and drive far from it the snares of the enemy;
may your holy angels dwell with us and guard
    us in peace,
and may your blessing be always upon us;
through Jesus Christ our Lord.
Amen.

PART 3

WINDRUSH –
THE
EXPERIENCE
OF PEOPLE
OF COLOUR IN
BRITAIN

THEOLOGICAL REFLECTION

by Chine McDonald

Chine McDonald is Director of the Theos Thinktank and is a regular contributor to Thought for the Day *on BBC Radio 4.*

When Lucille Anderson arrives in England from Jamaica in 1960, she is not prepared for the fact that she will be seen as a curiosity both in her workplace and her place of worship. A committed Christian raised by middle class parents in a place described as 'the most English town in Jamaica', like many of the Windrush generation, who answered the call of Minister of Health Enoch Powell to come to England and work, she felt a sense that England was 'home'.

As the first and only black nurse at Nonnatus House, she experiences what a lot of her colleagues don't – from a genuine curiosity from some of her patients who may not have been used to seeing a black person to more overt racism. For Lucille, such discrimination is confusing because it lies so contrary to the perception of herself as someone who hails from a nation that perceives England as 'the mother country'. It also completely contradicts the open arms with which people like Enoch Powell and the British government welcomed those from the Caribbean islands because they wanted them to help rebuild Britain's workforce and economy.

The ship Empire Windrush arrived at Tilbury Docks in Essex on 22 June 1948, bringing men, women and children from Jamaica, Trinidad and Tobago and other Caribbean islands. The term the Windrush Generation now refers to those arriving from those Caribbean countries between 1948 and 1971.

In Series 7, *Call the Midwife* begins to explore the particular issues faced by people of colour in the UK, including a storyline involving a Pakistani family and a sailor from Nigeria. Regardless of where they have come from, the individual stories of immigrants to the UK over the past few decades have had similar themes. People make the decision to move to the UK because they have aspirations about how they would like their lives to be and seek places where those opportunities lie. The Windrush generation felt a sense of duty to come help and rebuild the motherland. Many of those from the Caribbean left lives of relative comfort only to come to the UK and be made to feel unwelcome, facing hostility and discrimination.

This experience is a familiar one to my family. My mother, who worked in education, and my father, who was a doctor, made the decision to move with their three children from Nigeria to the UK. I sometimes wonder what it must have taken to leave the lives they had always known, their support network of family and friends, to move to a foreign country in the hopes of fulfilling their aspirations for themselves and their children. I know something of what Lucille Anderson felt coming to England and realising that she was black. When everyone else looks like you, you don't perceive of yourself as different or belonging to a certain race. In majority white spaces, it is understandable therefore that white people do not see their own whiteness and that it is non-white people who are expected to confirm. As Reni Eddo-Lodge writes in *Why I'm no Longer Talking to White People About Race*, 'To be white is to be human; to be white is universal. I only know this because I am not.'

One of the defining moments in my childhood was Stephen Lawrence's murder. I was nine years old when he was killed – and we were living in the town in which he was murdered – Eltham, in south-east London. For years afterwards, I couldn't walk past the bus stop where his life was so tragically cut short without thinking about him. His death changed the way that black immigrant families like mine felt about our new home. In an instant, it seemed we were no longer welcome. We felt vulnerable and conspicuous. We feared similar racist attacks on people we knew, people like us.

Stephen Lawrence's murder not only changed the atmosphere for those of us living in Eltham at the time, but in the 25 years that have followed, it has turned out to be a defining moment in our nation's history. The Macpherson report of 1999 into Stephen Lawrence's murder concluded that there was discrimination in the ranks which allowed the white racist gang suspected of his murder to walk free. The report from Her Majesty's Inspectorate of Constabulary and the Fire and Rescue Services found large-scale failings in the way hate crimes were dealt with.

In thinking about Lucille's experiences of otherness in *Call the Midwife,* it might be easier to stomach if we were to believe that her experiences are a thing of the past and that society has moved on. It would be easy to feel that racism, discrimination and prejudice are no longer issues a civilized society needs to deal with.

However, the truth is that 25 years after the Macpherson Report and decades since the Windrush generation arrived, many people of colour continue to face multiple forms of discrimination on a daily basis. In the health service, medical professionals are often made to feel, as one doctor put it in November 2019, 'worthless'. Dr Radhakrishna Shanbhag, a senior surgeon who had worked in the NHS for more than 20 years, shared how a patient had asked him, 'Can I have a white doctor?'[2] The revelations about the racism NHS workers face regularly prompted health secretary Matt Hancock to pen a letter to all NHS staff in which he said the racially-motivated incidents were 'shocking' and that the government took a 'zero tolerance' approach to racism.

Unfortunately, the existence of racism and prejudice does not come as a surprise to the many

---

2   *Telegraph, November 2019 https://www.telegraph.co.uk/ news/2019/11/06/nhs-workers-must-say-no-patients-ask- white-doctor-matt-hancock/*

people of colour who live in the UK – whether they were born here, or whether they migrated here at various points over the past few decades.

Many individual black people in the UK face regular instances of prejudice – from the relatively minor-microaggressions which make them feel like they are 'other' to the big systemic challenges that black and minority ethnic people face as a group. Asian and black households in the UK are more likely to be in persistent poverty, attainment of black Caribbean school pupils is lower than white British pupils, black men are three-and-a-half times more likely to be arrested than white men[3] and less likely to be represented in the corridors of power.

Racism is pervasive in society as a whole. But the heart-breaking thing is that it is also prevalent within the UK church – a space which is supposed to be a place of welcome and belonging in which the barriers between races and genders and generations are broken down. As we read in Ephesians 2:14: 'For he himself is our peace, who has made the two groups one and has destroyed the barrier, the dividing wall of hostility.' As an immigrant to the UK and a Christian, I sometimes reflect on how my family and I were received by the churches we attended. When you are a black family of five turning up at all-white churches in places like Hertfordshire or Kent or Hampshire, people notice. I recall my parents being

[3]   *Race Disparity Audit 2018 https://assets.publishing. service.gov.uk/government/uploads/system/uploads/attach- ment_data/file/686071/Rev'dised_RDA_report_March_2018. pdf*

asked once by a woman on the welcome team why they had chosen that particular church to attend instead of the black church down the road. I'm sure she thought her question was harmless, but I have never forgotten it. It suggested that not only did she see our race first rather than see us as members of God's big family – her family – but that the norm she had become accustomed to was that white people were in one place and black people were supposed to be in another. This view lies so contrary to the gospel – a gospel that breaks down divisions, between men and women, between slaves and free, between God and humanity.

We know that racism exists in society as a whole, but it is extremely disappointing that it is also pervasive in the Church. We've often heard it said that the Church remains one of the most racially segregated spaces in society. My experience as a black person in white majority spaces is that white is the norm and everything else symbolises difference and otherness.

As a black British person of African descent, the feelings I have about race and belonging and identity are extremely complicated. On one hand, I want my culture and heritage and background to be celebrated. I feel compelled not to conform to whiteness. On the other hand, I feel uncomfortable when I am marked out as different; when I am asked where I'm from by strangers keen to know my heritage just because I am not white. At times when I've thought about race issues within the Church, I've been met with a retort that says that all are equal under God and therefore we should not play into identity politics – in other words, I've been warned not to 'play the race card'.

As Christians, we need to recognise our brokenness and realise that each of us holds prejudices about others; each of us can at times draw boundaries that include some and exclude others; each of us is in danger of falling into the trap of 'single story'.

Lagos, the city in which I was born is Africa's most populous city. And so, from a young age, I was surrounded by people. Lagos is full of hustle and bustle. Its entrepreneurial spirit can be sensed as soon as you touch down at its airport – it clings to you like the sticky heat. But Lagos is not one-dimensional. As an African, I often find the generally one-dimensional depictions of the vast, sprawling, diverse and beautiful continent troubling. Narratives focus around – on one hand – its poverty and corruption; and on the other the assumption of unbridled joy despite having very little; painting yet again a simplistic African story. As the late great writer Chinua Achebe once said: 'People go to Africa and confirm what they already have in their heads and so they fail to see what is there in front of them.'

Before I moved to the UK with my parents when I was aged four, it never occurred to me that I was African. And, therefore, it had never occurred to me that people would have a story in their heads about me as soon as they saw me or heard my name. But from a very young age – from going to primary school in south-east London in the 1980s – I very soon discovered the stories that people had about

Africa, and therefore me, in their heads. 'Do you live in the jungle? Have you ever seen a lion? Did you have food to eat when you were in Africa?' Rather than the heterogeneous, wonderful diversity of Africa that I now know exists, I was reduced to one single story. Nigerian author Chimamanda Ngozi Adichie once said this in her TED talk on the danger of a single story: 'The single story creates stereotypes, and the problem with stereotypes is not that they are untrue, but that they are incomplete. They make the one story become the only story.' As humans we simplify each other into the stories that we have about each other. And we decide straight away whether another is one of us, or one of 'them'. An insider or an outsider.

For many of those who came to Britain on the Empire Windrush, their experience was of being outsiders; of being excluded rather than included. But in the Church it shouldn't just be about 'inclusion'. It should be 'a radical inclusion', regardless of where we have come from. We read in Ephesians 2:19-22:

'Consequently, you are no longer foreigners and strangers, but fellow citizens with God's people and also members of his household, built on the foundation of the apostles and prophets, with Christ Jesus himself as the chief cornerstone. In him the whole building is joined together and rises to become a holy temple in the Lord. And in him you too are being built together to become a dwelling in which God lives by his Spirit.'

Through this radical inclusion with Christ Jesus as the cornerstone, the passage describes how we are being built together – the barriers between us having been broken down - become a dwelling in which God lives by his Spirit. Radical racial reconciliation is a stunning reflection of the ultimate reconciliation that exists between humanity and God.

For people of colour like Lucille in *Call the Midwife,* the truth that God created humanity in all of its diversity speaks to us of our beauty, our value and the *imago dei* within us, rendering each of us worthy of inherent dignity, love, worth and respect.

COURSE
MATERIALS
by the Revd Rebecca Amoroso

Poplar, in the East End of London, was one of many areas of Britain that suffered devastating losses in World War II. This meant the active, working, population, needed to restore and sustain the country in the aftermath of war, was greatly depleted. The British government urgently needed people and so, offering attractive prospects and cheap passage, it called upon the people of the British Empire and Commonwealth to come and settle in Britain, the 'Mother Country'. On 22 June 1948, the ship 'Empire Windrush' docked at Tilbury docks bringing, among her passengers, many former servicemen from Kingston, Jamaica, eager to take up their citizenship of the UK. These people, and the many men and women that came after, came to be known as the 'Windrush Generation'. Sadly, these hopefuls were often faced with racism, discrimination, and intolerance, at times leading to violent clashes.

In 2018, the 'Windrush scandal' left many members of the 'Windrush generation' without benefits or healthcare, even refused re-entry to the UK, or threatened with deportation. This political scandal claimed many victims, including people who died as a direct or indirect result of this treatment. The government issued an apology, beginning to restore the rights of the people of Windrush, who helped restore Britain after the war.

This session explores some of the issues faced by the Windrush Generation, then and now, and is an opportunity to consider our response, as individuals, and as church.

OPENING PRAYER

A candle is lit and these words are said:

'This candle is to remind us of God's presence with us.'

Silence is kept.

OPTIONAL: WATCH CALL THE MIDWIFE *Series 7, episode 1, clip from 23.57 - 25.47: Lucille arrives in Poplar; and clip from 27.05 – 28.33: Lucille's first morning at Nonnatus House.*

INTRODUCTION

Group leaders may wish to read this out loud or introduce the theme in their own words.

During the winter of 1962 to1963, Britain was frozen. The 'Big Freeze' brought the country almost to a standstill, with weeks of heavy snowfall and freezing temperatures. Transport was halted, telephone lines cut off, and power-cuts disrupting all services. And still the babies of Poplar, in the East End of London, were being born. The midwives of *Call the Midwife's*

Nonnatus House, were continuing to provide vital nursing care in treacherous conditions, and, in desperate need of reinforcements, in the form of new midwife, Lucille.

In the dark, snow-filled street, a lone figure makes her way along the icy path, wrapped in a red scarf. She slips and falls on the ice, and as she rights herself, she is revealed as Lucille, the new midwife. Lucille is greeted cheerfully at the door and brought inside to have her cut knee cleaned and to be supplied with hot tea and brandy. In a small echo of the long journey of the Windrush Generation, Lucille explains that she has been 'travelling for two days' and had walked the last part of the journey after her train was evacuated. She tells the midwives that she trained in Taunton, 'quite a few of us arrived from the West Indies and went straight there', and shows her practical, fleece-lined boots. It is the first time she has had to wear them, although her mother must have been well aware of British weather when she sent Lucille the money to buy the boots.

This warm welcome, like that promised by the advertisements, was certainly not extended by all who encountered the people of Windrush. The inhospitable weather more closely reflects the experience of many, who received a far frostier reception. The other midwives are well aware of this, as their discussion the following morning demonstrates:

> Sister: What do you suppose our patients will say about her being … coloured?
> Mother: One would hope they won't say anything. There have been West Indian nurses at St Cuthbert's for some time.

Midwife: Nevertheless, people can be frightfully ignorant …

Midwife: Hm, and rude, especially round here …

Midwife: Anyone saying anything sideways deserves to be corrected. The National Health was struggling until all these girls started coming from the Commonwealth.

Lucille, despite being welcome at Nonnatus House, faces the obstacle of a hostile environment, as well as a 'rip-roaring bladder infection'. And she will face more challenges to come, as foreshadowed by the conversation at the breakfast table. Poplar, while desperately in need of well-qualified, practical and resourceful midwives like Lucille and the 'girls' from the Commonwealth, was not ready or prepared to receive them and the gifts they brought.

Lucille was welcome at Nonnatus House, though she faced, and still faces, a difficult journey. How does the church speak out against prejudice and discrimination, and demonstrate ways of peace and unity? How does the church support and encourage those who face hostility from others?

LECTIO DIVINA

Listen carefully as someone reads this passage from the Bible, then take some time afterwards to reflect in silence on what you have just heard.

The passage is provided in one translation here, you may wish to use a different version (visit Biblegateway.com to find alternative versions). Sometimes it is helpful to provide group members with a copy so that they can read along.

All of Life

1 CORINTHIANS 12:12-26 (NEW REVISED STANDARD VERSION)

For just as the body is one and has many members, and all the members of the body, though many, are one body, so it is with Christ. For in the one Spirit we were all baptized into one body — Jews or Greeks, slaves or free — and we were all made to drink of one Spirit.

Indeed, the body does not consist of one member but of many. If the foot were to say, 'Because I am not a hand, I do not belong to the body', that would not make it any less a part of the body. And if the ear were to say, 'Because I am not an eye, I do not belong to the body', that would not make it any less a part of the body. If the whole body were an eye, where would the hearing be? If the whole body were hearing, where would the sense of smell be? But as it is, God arranged the members in the body, each one of them, as he chose. If all were a single member, where would the body be? As it is, there are many members, yet one body. The eye cannot say to the hand, 'I have no need of you', nor again the head to the feet, 'I have no need of you.' On the contrary, the members of the body that seem to be weaker are indispensable, and those members of the body that we think less honourable we clothe with greater honour, and our less respectable members are treated with greater respect; whereas our more respectable members do not need this. But God has so arranged the body, giving the greater honour to the inferior member, that there may be no dissension within the body, but the members may have the same care for one another. If one member suffers, all suffer together with it; if one member is honoured, all rejoice together with it.

ℭ

- Listen again to the verses, read in a different voice.
- Is there a word, or a sentence, that jumps out at you? Which of these words are for you today? Why?
- Either in pairs or in the main group, share with each other the word or phrase that stood out.

Read through once more with a different reader. Has that word or phrase changed?

DISCUSSION TOPICS

Sometimes it can be difficult to start a conversation, especially on a sensitive topic. For the discussion part of the session we have provided a series of conversation starters. We have found the best way to run this part of the session is to photocopy the grid of questions, cut them out, fold and place in a bowl. Encourage group members to take a question, read it out and discuss as a group. The randomness of this can help people to open up more than if the 'leader' asks the questions directly.

Don't feel you have to try and 'answer' all the questions, the main aim is to have a fruitful and interesting discussion. Scan the questions first to see if any might be unhelpful or triggering for people in your group and exclude them. You can also leave the option to people to pass on a question if they wish.

You may wish also to write some discussion questions of your own on this theme that will suit your context. Ideally, this section of the session should feel relaxed and informal.

A midwife uses the word 'coloured' to describe Lucille. Why is this word, and others like it, unacceptable?

Does Lucille's determination to make her journey strike a chord with you? Why?

What effect do you think prejudice had, and has, on the Windrush Generation?

Do you think there is prejudice in the church?

Can you think of any examples of overcoming adversity that inspire you?

How does the church help you understand and overcome discrimination?

Have you ever recognised discrimination against another?

What did you do?

How have attitudes changed since 1948,
and have they changed enough?

'*I note the obvious differences
between each sort and type,
but we are more alike, my friends,
than we are unalike.*'
Maya Angelou, *Human Family*

How have *Call the Midwife* and other
people helped you to explore the effects
of prejudice and discrimination?

Have you a new or better understanding?

Have you ever been discriminated against?

How did you feel?

Have you ever felt prejudiced against
someone, and do you feel able to share?

RESPONSE TIME

Below are some suggestions for activities to respond to the Bible reading and group discussion. You may wish to use one or a few of these suggestions or come up with an idea of your own. Appropriate music could be played to encourage a prayerful atmosphere. You may wish to begin and end with a time of silence.

1. Create a word-cloud of words you associate with prejudice and discrimination.

2. Make a map or timeline of all the places you have visited or hope to visit in your lifetime.

3. Make a poster for your church that helps people to feel welcome, no matter who they are or what they look like.

4. In pairs, take two minutes each to observe and share, without interruption, the differences you observe between one another.

5. Write a letter to Lucille, or someone you know, to help them feel welcome in this place.

You may wish to close the response time by singing this chant or another suitable song:

> *In the Lord I'll be ever thankful;*
> *in the Lord I will rejoice.*
> *Look to God; do not be afraid.*
> *Lift up your voices the Lord is near;*
> *lift up your voices the Lord is near.*

(Taizé)

This session may have touched on some difficult, and personal themes.

Invite a time of stillness so that people can think about something that they have found challenging or an action they need to undertake in response to this session.

FINAL PRAYER

Spend some time in silent prayer praying for the person to your right. Then read this prayer in conclusion:

Visit this place, O Lord, we pray,
and drive far from it the snares of the enemy;
may your holy angels dwell with us and guard
us in peace,
and may your blessing be always upon us;
through Jesus Christ our Lord.
Amen.

PART 4

LGBTQIA+ PEOPLE – FROM INTOLERANCE TO ACCEPTANCE AND BEYOND

THEOLOGICAL REFLECTION

by the Revd Claire Jones

The Revd Claire Jones is in a civil partnership and is a priest in the Church of England.

The cultural calendar of the UK has expanded in recent years, as evidenced by the seasonal changes in supermarket displays. As well as the creepy costumes of Halloween, the festive food of Christmas, and the endless eggs of Easter, you'll now find vibrant rainbows appearing at their allotted time each year. While Pride parades pop up in increasing numbers of towns and cities across the country, you no longer have to attend a march to take part in the festivities. In June, designated as Pride month, everything from sandwich packets to mouthwash bottles gets branded in the distinctive stripes, as businesses fall over themselves to be seen celebrating the lesbian, gay, bisexual and trans (LGBTQIA+) community.

For a generation growing up with such apparent support of gender and sexual diversity, the attitudes to same-sex relations in 1950s and 1960s Britain seem entirely alien. How could it be that something which garners public and even commercial affirmation now could have been a criminal offence little more than 50 years ago? Of course, the picture both then and now is more complex than these generalisations suggest. Before 1967, female same-sex relations were not subject to the same criminalisation as those between men, and many of the freedoms now afforded to LGBTQIA+ people have been very recent victories; the armed forces only lifted the ban on openly LGBTQIA+ people serving in 2016. Social attitudes tend to be broader than legal proscriptions, and the stories of individuals can give a far more nuanced picture than facts and figures alone.

Through snapshot glimpses and deeper delves into the lives of a few characters, *Call the Midwife* explores the fears, dilemmas and occasional joys of what was a largely hidden community. Despite the huge societal shifts over the past half a century, these experiences strike resounding chords in the lives of many LGBTQIA+ Christians today. When the usually concealed bubbles of love and desire do rise to the surface in view of others, their reactions offer opportunity to reflect on our own engagement with the ongoing tensions faced by our LGBTQIA+ siblings, particularly within the life of the Church.

RISKY ENCOUNTERS

In Series 4, episode 3, we meet Tony Amos: on the surface, every bit the doting husband to his besotted wife. Successful at work and in family life, with a baby on the way, we believe that all is going well for

Mr Amos. But the illusion comes crumbling down in a matter of minutes. He is caught in a public toilet, about to engage in a sexual act with a stranger who turns out to be the bait in a police sting. Utter desperation fills Tony's voice as he is arrested, and it becomes clear why.

When Mrs Marie Amos hears the news, she initially enters a horrified state of denial, adamant that she could never have fallen for someone 'so unnatural'. She later seeks reassurance that it was an isolated incident, but this too is an illusion. Eventually, after Tony has been found guilty of the criminal act but spared jail, the truth is painfully articulated between them. She cries, 'You can't even kiss me without closing your eyes. You think I don't see that?' Tony plans to leave, but Marie will hear nothing of it. He must 'be a man now ... take your punishment and get cured, because you ain't going nowhere.' With no way of escape, and distraught at the prospect of female hormones to 'cure him', Tony attempts suicide.

The turmoil of Tony Amos illustrates the pressure cooker environment in which gay men were driven to such risky behaviour. 'Cottaging' (anonymous sex between men in public toilets) still exists in some parts of male gay culture, and promiscuity is a stereotype still associated with this group. But the stereotypes do nothing to uncover the depths of pain and loneliness experienced by those who had no other outlet available to them.

Although the law has changed and cultural attitudes have shifted, the lived reality for

LGBTQIA+ people – especially those from religious or culturally conservative backgrounds – may not be so far from that of Tony Amos. A sense of being trapped by social expectations, the weight of shame and self-hatred, and the ostracism by family and community networks still forces many into clandestine encounters which put them at risk of exploitation or harm.

The need for change runs as an undercurrent throughout the Amos' storyline. Dr Turner, who provides a sympathetic character reference for Tony in court, argues that his patient badly wants to change and that medical treatment is possible. With the prospect of jail looming, we may understand how such intervention appeared to be a compassionate response to the plight of gay men in the 1950s and 60s. But despite his thankfulness for this mercy in court, Tony Amos is disturbed by the prospect, telling his wife, 'They're giving me women's hormones. Don't you understand? I won't be the same,' he says. 'I don't want you to be the same,' she replies. 'Enough Tony. Got to forget all this now. It's a new start.'

In more recent decades, scientific research has shown reparative therapy, or conversion therapy, to be ineffective at changing a person's orientation, harmful to those who undertake it, and wholly unnecessary – homosexuality is no longer considered a medical condition or mental disorder but an entirely natural variation in the human species. In 2017 the Church of England's General Synod called for a ban on the practice of conversion therapy, and a year later, the UK Government announced plans to do so.

A desperate need for change was experienced by the fictional Tony Amos and the real lives represented in his story. But it has never been the attractions of gay, lesbian and bisexual people that needed alteration; rather it was the legal status, scientific understanding, and social attitudes towards same-sex relationships. It is easy to be complacent today, believing that the major developments required in UK law and culture have largely been achieved. But listening to the contemporary stories of LGBTQIA+ people in our churches and communities soon highlights how much work there is still to be done.

For churches who seek to offer a welcome to people from across the LGBTQIA+ spectrum, the conviction of Tony Amos offers a firm challenge. Truly inclusive churches must expect to welcome those who have engaged (and may still do so) in all manner of risky sexual behaviours without a hint of judgement or condemnation. Of course, wherever Christian faith grows in any person, their sexual ethics may well change, and the expression of their sexuality might alter. But extra care is needed to avoid any implication that a person's sexual orientation can or should be changed. Many LGBTQIA+ folk who have had contact with church will have a heightened sensitivity to these sentiments, often dressed up in seemingly innocuous statements such as 'We're all sinners'. When we have the privilege of meeting those who have lived with the fear of rejection from their families, churches have a real opportunity to offer safety, love and true acceptance.

SECRECY AND STATUS

For those with eyes to see, nurse Patsy Mount finds the whole incident with Tony Amos more unnerving than the other midwives and Sisters of Nonnatus House. She pays quiet but careful attention to their reactions and attitudes to the offence, and we begin to understand that this is because of the nature of her own relationship with fellow nurse, Delia Busby.

Patsy and Delia are introduced as old friends, but it is clear that their feelings for one another are of a romantic nature. Over cosy chats in a local café, the two women share their deep frustrations at the limitations of their relationship. When Patsy asks in surprise if Delia really wants to conform to the social norm of marriage, she replies, 'Yes, more than anything. To you, you fool. But I can't, and that's that.' Still, as two single women, their situation is more tolerable than that of Tony Amos. They are able to move into a flat together as friends, because as Delia says, 'not even a nun would bat an eyelid' at two women cohabiting.

This kind of compromise will be familiar for many LGBTQIA+ people and their partners, who over the decades have found ways to quietly enjoy domestic life together while keeping the nature of their relationship private. Such secrecy may not be necessary for many couples today, with many feeling able to be public about their sexuality. But the decision to 'come out' is not a one-off event and requires a weighing up the choices in varying contexts, even multiple times a day. When a colleague or acquaintance assumes your partner is of a different gender, there is a split-second in which to choose whether to correct the pronouns or let the assumption pass. It entails fast judgements about the possible consequences of revealing this information, and readiness to deal with negative reactions ranging from awkwardness to aggression.

But secrecy is not the only frustration facing Patsy and Delia. No sooner are they happily installed in their new flat, basic and bare but brimming with joyful potential, tragedy strikes. A bicycle accident leaves Delia concussed, and the hospital will give Patsy no information about her condition because she is not the next of kin. When she visits the hospital and meets Delia's mother, Patsy is acknowledged by Mrs Busby only as 'the lady she helps with cubs'. The lack of privileged status as Delia's partner is the external symptom; there is evidently a deep inward pain at not having the intimacy of their relationship recognised by others. The distress is exacerbated further when it becomes apparent that Delia has lost her memory of friends and family, and therefore does not recognise Patsy; she is taken home by her parents to recuperate and Patsy has little hope of maintaining meaningful contact with her.

The status of same-sex partners is still contested territory, despite the change in UK law to extend marriage to same-sex couples in 2014. When British man David Bulmer-Rizzi tragically died in Australia in 2016, his death certificate first listed him as 'never married', despite being on his honeymoon with husband Marco at the time of his death. After the inevitable uproar, the decision was reversed, and Australia went on to legalise same-sex marriage in 2017. The total number of countries in which it is possible stands at 28, at the time of writing. But legal possibilities do not tell the whole story, and there remain social and cultural barriers which deny some same-sex couples a status entirely equal to their heterosexual friends.

For instance, the Church of England, in which I am called to serve, forbids its ordained ministers from entering same-sex marriages. Civil partnerships are allowed on the condition that they are celibate relationships, and priests must be prepared to give clear assurances to their bishops that this is the case. Even so, there plenty of congregations in the Church of England which maintain a theological objection to same-sex couplings of any kind. So those in civil partnerships who abide by the conditions are still excluded from a great many churches in which they might otherwise apply to minister.

The compromised situation of such clergy, who enjoy the legal recognition of their civil partnerships while being denied the full social status of a marriage, can result in a dilemma around terminology. In my own experience, close friends and family are likely to refer to Rose as my 'wife', recognising the exclusive, lifelong and public commitment we have made to one another. But having chosen to do this by a civil partnership rather than a marriage out of obedience to the Church's House of Bishops, I am conscious not to muddy the waters in the language I use. So particularly in a church context, I choose 'partner', or simply use her name. The problem is that 'partner' is a far more generic term and can leave people unsure about how they should refer to Rose. I have often listened to supportive and well-meaning people fumble around for a word to use and eventually settle on 'your friend'. Even as I try to relieve their awkwardness, I feel the sting of Patsy's pain, as in a single phrase the significance of my relationship is unintentionally diminished and denied.

But for every quietly jarring experience, there are many that uphold and celebrate our love. It is not always the overt symbols of inclusivity, like rainbow flags and Pride parades, which best make for a welcoming church. The most affirming encounters I have had are those in which someone asks after Rose just as they would ask after a husband. Simple questions like, 'Did you both enjoy your holiday?' or 'How is Rose finding her work?' fill me with joy at their normality and set me chattering happily about our very ordinary domestic life.

It really is that easy to play a part in undoing the negative experiences faced by LGBTQIA+ couples. If you know someone in your family, church or community with a same-sex partner, make a point of using their name and finding out what descriptor they are most comfortable with. Be explicit in letting them know that their boyfriend, wife, or partner, is welcome at church events; invite the two of them around for dinner and take an interest in their shared life. In doing so, you restore to their relationship the dignity and status it might otherwise be denied.

A TIME TO SPEAK

At a personal level, the full inclusion of LGBTQIA+ individuals, couples and families in the life of a church is a powerful witness to the God of welcome and love. But some will perceive that a Christian response to these issues requires more than quiet affirmation.

In the discussions about Tony Amos's actions that arise throughout Nonnatus House, Trixie often gives voice to a progressive viewpoint. She tells a story of having provided cover for a gay man during her training, and insists that telling people who they can and can't love is 'fascism'. But when a worried Patsy asks her, 'Am I the only one who doesn't despise … the queers?', Trixie replies 'Of course not. I just don't think it's our battle to fight.' This is a sentiment that is echoed by quietly supportive Christians across the country today. With so many important issues to campaign for, and the contentious nature of LGBTQIA+ issues in both Christian and wider culture, there are plenty of reasons not to weigh in on the subject.

But towards the end of the saga, Trixie finds that duty calls. Tony shows up at the community centre to insist that his wife will be taking her place in the Rose Queen pageant, defying the homophobic abuse they have faced. His boldness moves Trixie to speak up for him, declaring, 'Didn't Jesus tell us to love everyone, even the sinners?' Her fiancé, the curate, agrees: 'Especially the sinners.' Although progressive theology has moved far beyond referring to LGBTQIA+ people as sinners, the act of speaking up for a marginalised group makes an enormous difference. Voices of supportive 'allies' free up those under attack from having to defend themselves, and counters the sense of isolation and exclusion.

Moving towards a more public expression of support is a brave and often controversial step for a church. There will likely be those internally who 'just don't think it's our battle to fight', and external condemnation from other Christians theologically opposed to such advocacy. But if your church is quietly supportive of the rights of LGBTQIA+ people to live and love in peace, perhaps it is time to begin the conversation about a more vocal affirmation of these rights. For the LGBTQIA+ folks in your midst – whether known to you, or not yet 'out', confident in their identity or wrestling with shame – your collective voice could make all the difference.

COURSE MATERIALS

by the Revd Bryony Taylor

LGBT is the most commonly used abbreviation for Lesbian, Gay, Bisexual, and Trans people and is an umbrella term that is often used to refer to the community as a whole. Some people use LGBTQIA+ to intentionally include and raise awareness of Queer, Intersex and Asexual as well as myriad other communities. In this guide we will use LGBTQIA+ .

This session is an opportunity to explore how attitudes to LGBTQIA+ people have changed over the years, where there are still problems in society (such as conversion therapy) and what people in churches can learn and do to understand the LGBTQIA+ experience.

OPENING PRAYER

A candle is lit and these words are said:

'This candle is to remind us of God's presence with us.'

Silence is kept.

OPTIONAL: WATCH CALL THE MIDWIFE

Watch Series 4, episode 3, clip from 29.10-30.29 – a man receives a prescription for tablets to cure his homosexuality or Series 6, episode 8 clip from 49.15 to the end – Patsy and Delia finally kiss at the end of Series 6.

INTRODUCTION

Group leaders may wish to read this out loud or introduce the theme in their own words.

Set during the 1950s and 1960s the people in *Call the Midwife* live in an environment where homosexuality is seen as both an illness and, when it involves sexual activity, a criminal act. Across the series we encounter a couple of storylines. The first is that of an expectant father who is entrapped in a public toilet about to commit an 'indecent' act with an undercover policeman. He is ordered by a court to undergo medical treatment for his 'illness' and on his visit to the GP, he is told:

'There are other treatments, ECT, aversion therapy, but I'd say this is less brutal, and more private.'

He is offered tablets that contain oestrogen that will 'suppress his urges' but will also cause impotence and may make him grow breasts and lose hair. The man's tearful wife responds:

'Well it's not prison, and that's all that matters.'

This is an understated scene that only serves to heighten the emotions in the viewer of the brutal way in which society used to approach homosexuality particularly in men.

The second storyline, although bittersweet, has a happier outcome. Two of the midwives, Patsy and Delia, fall in love, but of course have to keep their relationship a secret. Their love for one another develops over two years and at the end of Series 6, we finally see them kiss.

The experience and acceptance of lesbian, gay, bisexual and trans people in the Britain has changed dramatically in the last 50 years. In terms of public policy we have moved from homosexual activity between consenting males being a crime, to Section 28 – a ruling that homosexuality was not to be 'promoted' in schools as a 'pretended family relationship' (finally repealed in 2003) to marriage equality being granted in 2013 in England and Wales, 2014 in Scotland and 2020 in Northern Ireland. Quite a journey of acceptance in quite a short space of time. The scenes shown in *Call the Midwife* are, for many, within living memory. Watching the scenes of a gay man being prescribed drugs to try and help him with his 'illness' only serves to show how far we have come.

But how far have public attitudes shifted, especially in the church? How can we as Christians respond to and welcome people who identify as lesbian, gay, bisexual, trans, queer, questioning or asexual?

LECTIO DIVINA

Listen carefully as someone reads this passage from the Bible, then take some time afterwards to reflect in silence on what you have just heard.

The passage is provided in one translation

here, you may wish to use a different version (visit Biblegateway.com to find alternative versions). Sometimes it is helpful to provide group members with a copy so that they can read along.

EPHESIANS 2:14-22 [NEW REVISED STANDARD VERSION]

For he is our peace; in his flesh he has made both groups into one and has broken down the dividing wall, that is, the hostility between us. He has abolished the law with its commandments and ordinances, so that he might create in himself one new humanity in place of the two, thus making peace, and might reconcile both groups to God in one body through the cross, thus putting to death that hostility through it. So he came and proclaimed peace to you who were far off and peace to those who were near; for through him both of us have access in one Spirit to the Father. So then you are no longer strangers and aliens, but you are citizens with the saints and also members of the household of God, built upon the foundation of the apostles and prophets, with Christ Jesus himself as the cornerstone. In him the whole structure is joined together and grows into a holy temple in the Lord; in whom you also are built together spiritually into a dwelling-place for God.

℘

- Listen again to the verses, read in a different voice.
- Is there a word, or a sentence, that jumps out at you? Which of these words are for you today?

Why?

- Either in pairs or in the main group, share with each other the word or phrase that stood out.

Read through once more with a different reader. Has that word or phrase changed?

DISCUSSION TOPICS

Sometimes it can be difficult to start a conversation, especially on a sensitive topic. For the discussion part of the session we have provided a series of conversation starters. We have found the best way to run this part of the session is to photocopy the grid of questions, cut them out, fold and place in a bowl. Encourage group members to take a question, read it out and discuss as a group. The randomness of this can help people to open up more than if the 'leader' asks the questions directly.

Don't feel you have to try and 'answer' all the questions, the main aim is to have a fruitful and interesting discussion. Scan the questions first to see if any might be unhelpful or triggering for people in your group and exclude them. You can also leave the option to people to pass on a question if they wish.

You may wish also to write some discussion questions of your own on this theme that will suit your context. Ideally, this section of the session should feel relaxed and informal.

In what ways is **Patsy and Delia's** love story the same and different from a heterosexual relationship?

'Love is love.'

What do you think about this expression?

Is it true?

What did treating sexuality as an illness do to gay people in the past?

How might an **LGBTQIA+** person feel excluded in church?

What do you find your identity in?

'All are welcome' – most churches say this, but how do we make sure it is really true – especially when thinking about the **LGBTQIA+** community?

Have you or anyone you know experienced discrimination because of their sexuality?

Share a story if you feel comfortable

How has your attitude to **LGBTQIA+ people** changed over the years? Why?

'You never really understand a person until you consider things from his point of view ... Until you climb inside of his skin and walk around in it.' Harper Lee, *To Kill a Mockingbird*

Is it true?
How has *Call the Midwife* and other people helped you to understand the **LGBTQIA+** experience? Has it changed your perspective?

What one thing do you think the church could do to be more open to **LGBTQIA+** people?

Does the church need to repent of its treatment of **LGBTQIA+** people?

RESPONSE TIME

Below are some suggestions for activities to respond to the Bible reading and group discussion. You may wish to use one or a few of these suggestions or come up with an idea of your own. Appropriate music could be played to encourage a prayerful atmosphere. You may wish to begin and end with a time of silence.

1. Draw on a large piece of paper a series of bricks, write on those bricks the things that cause division in our community. Then paint a brightly coloured cross in the centre of the wall to show that through the cross, Jesus has broken down the wall that divides us from each other.

2. Create a 'wailing wall' prayer activity – take some hardboard (at least a metre square in size). Draw some bricks onto the wall and then drill small holes (1cm wide) all over it in the 'cracks'. Supply some small pieces of paper on which people can write their prayers. In secret they can roll their prayers and place them in the holes in the wall. You may wish to play some music during this prayer time.

3. Kintsugi Craft. Kintsukuroi is the Japanese art of repairing broken pottery with gold or silver so that the pot is more beautiful for having been broken. Some beautiful images of this can be seen online.

    For this activity you will need some gold and silver metallic card, some plain grey or white sugar paper, scissors and glue sticks. Give each person a pot shape cut from the grey sugar paper. Tell them to cut the pot into pieces, thinking about how their lives have been broken at times. Then each person reassembles their pot, sticking the pieces to the metallic card. The final result should look something like this:

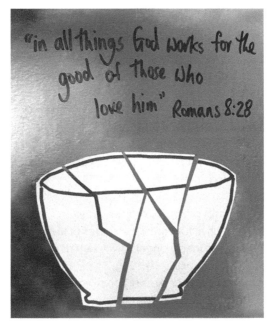

4. Create an LGBTQIA+ friendly welcome banner for your church or to carry at a Pride event near you.

You may wish to close the response time by singing this chant or another suitable song:

In the Lord I'll be ever thankful;
in the Lord I will rejoice.
Look to God; do not be afraid.
Lift up your voices the Lord is near;
lift up your voices the Lord is near.

(Taizé)

This session may have touched on some difficult, and personal themes.

Invite a time of stillness so that people can think about something that they have found challenging or an action they need to undertake in response to this session.

FINAL PRAYER

Spend some time in silent prayer praying for the person to your right. Then read this prayer in conclusion:

Visit this place, O Lord, we pray,
and drive far from it the snares of the enemy;
may your holy angels dwell with us and guard
    us in peace,
and may your blessing be always upon us;
through Jesus Christ our Lord.
Amen.

PART 5

VOCATION AND CALLING

THEOLOGICAL REFLECTION

by the Revd Frances Wilson

Mother Frances Wilson is a Priest working at Marygate House on Holy Island; previously she served as Bishops' Director of Ordinands in Lichfield Diocese.

'*Why did I ever start this…?*'

Into the bustling, noisy, male world of an East End dockyard, a stylish young woman in high heels and a pale tailored skirt treads, astonished and nervous. As she enters the darker tenements, the place of the women and children, she muses: 'I could have been an air hostess; I could have been a model; I could have moved to Paris, or become a concert pianist … I side-stepped love and set off for the East End of London.'

As she nears Nonnatus House, her way is blocked by two dirty and untidy women. Later we will find that one of these women, Pearl, has syphilis, presumably caught from her husband's visits to the woman with whom she has been fighting. Nurse Lee, seen later frantically scrubbing her hands in revulsion at what she has found, is offered her first lesson in her new life: Sister Julienne tells her, 'Pearl is not used to caring, or even being cared for.' Jenny has side-stepped love, but Pearl has never been loved or valued.

Like all good opening scenes, important themes are laid bare: love and being loved, opportunity and challenge; and how this affects our ability to know and fulfil what God calls us to achieve and become.

The Sisters of the Order of St Raymond Nonnatus (literally 'not born'; 'Happy survivor of caesarean section', Sister Monica Joan informs the newly-arrived Nurse Lee) is a pseudonym for the Society of Saint John the Evangelist (SSJE), a community which was itself born into the East End of London in 1848 to care for those living in poverty there. Like the Sisters of SSJE, the Sisters we meet in this series are a mixed bunch!

Sister Monica Joan meets Jenny Lee at the door and welcomes us into the inner life of a Religious Community. Whisking her off to the kitchen, we see what a warm and welcoming Sister she is (often seen in the background at the busy mother and baby clinics, playing with a Sooty puppet or giving out sweets to children, who obviously like her) – and what a pest she must be to live with! She is the cake thief from whom the Sisters must hide the baking. She is highly intelligent (often quoting obscure classical writers), at times preferring the company of her books to that of her Sisters; she prays (and how often, when a midwife or family are in the midst of a difficult or frightening situation, does the camera move from it to the Sisters praying, singing hymns and reciting the Psalms) and she tries to help. She worries that she is losing her mind, whether she still has a purpose in living in Poplar – and she worries her Sisters! She can get lost in her confusion and she has been known to steal small items from local stallholders.

Born with a 'silver spoon in her mouth', of a well-to-do family, her background and character is a world away from that of Sister Evangelina. It is Cynthia who, when Jenny is shocked by the matter-of-fact way in which Sister Evangelina accepts the living standards of the families in Poplar, lets on that she grew up in extreme poverty herself. This makes her down-to-earth, practical; and at times tough, critical and judgemental.

Sister Evangelina and Sister Monica Joan often found each other difficult to live with: 'She may be my Sister-in-Christ but I swear she would drive a Methodist to drink!' says Sister Evangelina. However, when Sister Monica Joan goes missing at Christmas following a sharp exchange, it is Sister Evangelina who is distraught, and who is the one who guesses where she would find her. Likewise, it is Sister Monica Joan who knows how to get Sister Evangelina to accept that she needs medical treatment, in warning that otherwise she would be disqualified from work.

There are 'callings' which we consider special (even when we wouldn't want that calling for ourselves); nuns and monks are such people. 'How holy and good', we think they must be! Being given this inside look into the Community of St Raymond should cure us of this. Whenever we live out the life God shaped us to fulfil, it will 'fit' us and we will be the best we are meant to be.

Most of us don't see our future lit up in flashing lights or spoken to us directly in prayer. The Christmas Special which begins Series 3 shows us Cynthia, struggling to decide whether she should be a Sister. Often a person feels s/he is 'unworthy' of the vocation to which they believe God is calling them; 'How could God be calling *me* to be a ….' Because something is our heart's desire, we can't believe God could be so generous as to wish this for us. Wrestling with these thoughts, it is the unconditional love of a couple (both with mental health issues that make everyday existence difficult), who teach Cynthia that God doesn't require anything from us but our love and our desire. This, though, isn't the end of Cynthia's vocational journey; rather it is the beginning of a new chapter. She will go to the Mother House, where there are more of the Sisters to share this new life with, and the place of the Novitiate (where Novices – learners – live together) and return, still a Novice, to learn about being a nurse and a midwife *and* a Sister.

Living cheek-by-jowl with the Sisters are the midwives; the early series of *Call the Midwife* are an adaptation of Jennifer Worth's (Jenny Lee's) autobiography. If Jenny arrived at Nonnatus House by accident (which is not, as she expects, a private nursing home but a convent), the next new arrival, Chummy (Camilla Fortescue-Cholmondeley-Browne), has made a definite choice to work in the East End amongst the most needy, something Sister Evangelina bristles at, stating that she is just using them; district nursing and midwifery were merely 'stepping stones' for her. While Jenny professes no faith when asked by Sister Julienne on arrival ('Not really; I'm Church of England'), Chummy prays as she holds the cross around her neck for guidance and actively lives out her Christian faith.

Chummy soon settles into midwifery in Poplar, falling in love with a local policeman and marrying at the end of the first series. However, that first sense of being called to be a missionary won't go away. It is her husband, Peter, who applies on her behalf for the post in Sierra Leone but when he looks to join the local police force there, in order to accompany her, he finds he must complete a strenuous physical exam. It is the first test of Chummy's inner conviction, and an important one. God does not call a person to do something which is contradictory to the essential person God has created them to be; if Chummy and Peter's marriage was God-given, then this next vocation, to be a missionary, will work for both of them too. If not, then perhaps the interpretation of that inner voice was not correct, or incomplete.

Chummy meets with Sister Julienne to tell her that she and Peter are bound for Africa; she is obviously still unsure of herself, her abilities; and that her dream has involved extra work and worry for her husband. Sister Julienne reassures her: 'I generally find the Lord only asks of us what he knows we can give.' 'What if the Lord is wrong?' asks Chummy. 'Then we should all be very afraid'! It is not until part way through the next series that we get a final glimpse of the testing of Chummy's vocation: the Reverend Applebee-Thornton, newly returned from Sierra Leone reflects, 'It is my belief that

Nurse Noakes's calling came from her humanity as much as it did the Lord God almighty.' Chummy's longing to be a missionary, glimpsed at when she first arrives as Nonnatus House, is tested as a true vocation for her by the way it fits her personality, her circumstances (including her marriage) and in talking to others; through this careful discernment, her time in Sierra Leone has been a blessing to her and the people among whom she works.

There is a 'Call' on our lives, a vocation for which God has formed us, and there are 'callings', the different paths this Call takes us on. The Christmas Special, that opens Series 4, begins not in Poplar in 1959 but in the home of the retired Jenny Lee. Frustrated that she can't find the sheep, a long-ago gift from the Nonnatus House crib, she wonders, 'I'm not sure if I'm a fool, or a romantic or a creature of routine,' 'Last two,' says her husband, 'Once a nurse, always a nurse.'

Her love of midwifery is a golden theme running through *Call the Midwife;* 'Midwifery is the stuff of life,' the older Jenny reflects as she remembers her younger self entering Poplar for the first time. She certainly sees life in all its fullness – and loves to do so – in the life she shares with us, the viewers. When a friend from her past, Jimmy, asks whether she might grow more fond of him, think of him rather as a boyfriend, she replies, 'I've grown to love nursing more and more. I find myself feeling quite passionate about it; what I can learn, what I can achieve. It's become the thing that matters most to me.' And although when she finds out some time later that Jimmy is now unavailable, about to be

118

married, her assurance wavers, her single-minded following of her call to midwifery does not change until she falls in love – and the new love, Alec, dies in a fatal accident. 'I loved my work and the freedom that it brought me. I loved the teeming streets, the families I encountered; I loved it all. And I thought the joy would last forever.' It clearly did. These memoirs of Jenny Lee are full of her love of nursing, but as the door to her vocation as a midwife closed on her (as she so graphically felt on returning to work after compassionate leave, failing to be able to stay with a mother about to give birth), new doors opened; the meeting of the love of her life and her new calling to nurse in end-of-life care, hospice work.

Love, security and affirmation are pre-requisites for anyone to be able to fulfil their vocation; where these are lacking, a person can be squeezed into a way of life which is unhealthy, limiting or sad. Mary is a young girl who, running away from her home in rural Ireland, has been picked up by a pimp and works as a prostitute. Pregnant, she longs to keep her child; on the child's birth it is as if, she tells Jenny, '[I had been] missing her my whole life.' Some time later, Jenny receives a letter from Mary, distraught that her baby had been taken from her. An angry Jenny confronts Father Joe who has arranged for this to happen. He explains that she's only 15, not fit or ready to be a mother and could neither provide for herself and her child. Loveless in childhood and abused as a teenager, her opportunity to follow her calling to be a mother is deemed impossible.

Men must be men and work, and women must

be mothers. Hoping, dreaming and feeling called to something different is shown in all its riskiness. Tony Adams, a clean, rugged car mechanic has a pregnant wife when he is caught 'cottaging.' How can he be homosexual and married? Shelagh asks her husband Patrick, the doctor. 'I suppose it's how we've made things. A man gets married; he has a family. There isn't much room for a different way.'

Wilma Goddens already has her three daughters and with the youngest now old enough to spend days with a sitter, she wants to get back to work. She's got a new job as a corsetière with Constanza and she brims with excitement; she is good at it and has quickly become the highest grossing salesperson in the East End. The new contraceptive pill will enable her to put pregnancy behind her but her fear of her husband finding out is fatal; the cause of the pulmonary embolism she suffers (a side effect of the 'pill') is not known and she dies with her husband and girls around her hospital bed.

Vocation and call is not only something we discern, wrestle with, in our own lives. Loving, affirming, challenging (both individuals and the society in which we live, which still limits choice for some people), we will call out others to fulfil the vocation to which they are also called.

I hope that by now some 'myths' about Calling have been exploded for you: Calling isn't just for nuns and vicars! It's not only 'church work' but all that we are and do; it's not dull, hard work but something which is fulfilling (and will be fun, though not always!); it's not pre-determined

(God gives us choices) and we don't always see what God is calling us to do and be; our calling isn't once-for-all, it will change through our lives (and it's never too late to be called by God; some vocations are closed, but other options open up) and it will 'fit' who you are as a person and the people whom you love and with whom you share your life (remember Chummy and Peter).

So, what about you? Four questions to focus your mind on: 'What?', 'Who for?', 'How?' and 'Who with'?

- **What?** Jenny and the other midwives enjoy life! The work is long, and it's stretching and exhausting, but it fulfils them. What gives you life (and what drains you!); what fascinates you; what do you really care about; what are you good at; for what do you want people to remember you?
- **Who for?** Chummy found her feet (and her husband) in Poplar, but she dreamt of being a missionary. The Sisters were founded to serve the poor of the East End and made a huge difference to the lives of countless families. What sort of people do you enjoy working with, want to help; where could your presence make a difference; and where in the world would you wish to do that?
- **How?** Sister Winifred learnt to enjoy being a midwife with the help of Cynthia, but she was at her best when teaching (teaching children to clean their teeth, for instance). What are your gifts and talents, the way your brain works?

(And if that's a difficult question for you to answer, ask a friend.)

- **Who with?** A difficult labour; in Nonnatus House the Sisters are praying. When a child is lost; in Nonnatus House the Night Prayer is said. Tired and uneasy, the midwives slip into the Evening Prayer sung at Nonnatus House. We are rarely called to make our vocational journey alone. Who else shares your interest; 'gets you'; works well with you; whose skills and interests complement your own; who is doing the work you wish to do?

Gathering the answers to these questions together and sifting through them with a wise friend or spiritual guide will start to focus the mind on the area of work you are uniquely called and gifted to fulfil.

And finally, the beginning and the end of this reflection on *Call the Midwife* is that love and being loved is vital to the sense of self-worth which is able to believe that God is calling us, you, me. Opportunity and challenge are only possible when we know that we are loved, precious and worthy; if you feel that none of this is for you, that God would not call you, then seek out the help you need to know you are loved. If you do know that you are unique and loved, then help break down the barriers to ensure others do too.

COURSE MATERIALS

by the Revd Rebecca Amoroso

Vocation and calling are the words we use to describe a strong inclination or sense of 'pull' towards a particular way of life or work. Specifically, we use these word to describe a 'calling' to ministry or the religious life of a monk or nun, but we also use the term more broadly for a powerful sense of 'rightness' towards or in any state or occupation, e.g. a vocation to marriage, or a calling to teach.

This session is an opportunity to explore vocation and calling: what they mean in our lives, and what they mean in the life of the church.

OPENING PRAYER

A candle is lit and these words are said:

'This candle is to remind us of God's presence with us.'

Silence is kept.

OPTIONAL: WATCH CALL THE MIDWIFE
Watch Series 1, episode 1, clip from 50.28- 47.01: Jenny arrives in Poplar.

INTRODUCTION

Group leaders may wish to read this out loud or introduce the theme in their own words.

Call the Midwife is set in Poplar, in the East End of London, during the 1950s and 1960s. This area was still suffering the effects of heavy bombing during the Second World War, and many streets had become building sites as repair work was underway. Poverty was rife, and housing conditions cramped and squalid. These conditions led to poor hygiene and disease, and high rates of violence and crime.

Jenny is a well-spoken, well-educated young woman, who has arrived in the East End to work as a midwife. This is her first experience of Poplar, and she could not be more horrified by the scenes that greet her. As Jenny makes her way to Nonnatus House, where she is to work, she thinks aloud:

'I must have been mad. I could have been an air hostess. I could have been a model. I could have moved to Paris; or been a concert pianist. I could have seen the world, been brave, followed my heart. But I didn't. I side-stepped love, and set off for the East End of London, because I thought it would be easier. Madness is the only explanation.'

Jenny seems unable to explain exactly what has brought her to these grimy, noisy, rubble-filled streets. She expresses a combination of regret and fear, of all the things she could have done and been, and the unknown future that lies ahead. Jenny has arrived somewhere completely unexpected and alien to her.

As Jenny continues to reflect, her next words contrast with those first thoughts:

'Midwifery is the very stuff of life. Every child is conceived in love, or lust, and born in pain, followed by joy, or by tragedy and anguish. Every birth is attended by a midwife. She is in the thick of it, she sees it all.'

Jenny's first words were full of fear, but now she sounds sure; doubt has been replaced with certainty as she speaks of the vocation she is growing into – the vocation to nursing and midwifery.

Jenny knows already that this will not be an easy, or comfortable experience. She knocks at the door of Nonnatus House, and Sister Monica Joan answers the door, resulting in the following exchange:

> Sister: Venus and Saturn are now in alignment; it is entirely appropriate that you should appear. Welcome to Nonnatus House. What do you suppose that is? One hears of visitors from realms apart from ours.
> Jenny: I think it's an aeroplane.
> Sister: From the extreme height of your heels, I deduce that you are not a nun.
> Jenny: Are you a nun?
> Sister: We are the Sisters of St Raymond Nonnatus, midwives and district nurses, present at life's commencement, and at its end ...'

Sister Monica Joan's strange words reinforce the sense of dislocation and unease that Jenny is feeling. The Sister speaks of aliens from other realms, and to Jenny it seems as if she has landed on a different planet. With her high heels and smart suit, Jenny looks as unprepared as she feels for what will come next. But the Sister's last words echo Jenny's, and her sense of calling and vocation is affirmed.

Vocation and calling can seem a romantic notion, but the reality is often very different. Because we cannot control or determine our vocation or call, we can be left feeling a whole range of emotions, from regret to fear to shock and even anger, but also love and joy, fulfilment and satisfaction.

Jenny's vocation was supported and affirmed in Nonnatus House, in spite of challenging beginnings. How does the church support and affirm vocation, to all kinds of ministry and ways of life? How does the church support and encourage you?

LECTIO DIVINA

Listen carefully as someone reads this passage from the Bible, then take some time afterwards to reflect in silence on what you have just heard.

The passage is provided in one translation here, you may wish to use a different version (visit Biblegateway.com to find alternative versions). Sometimes it is helpful to provide group members with a copy so that they can read along.

ISAIAH 6:1-8 [NEW REVISED STANDARD VERSION]

In the year that King Uzziah died, I saw the Lord sitting on a throne, high and lofty; and the hem of his robe filled the temple. Seraphs were in attendance above him; each had six wings: with two they covered their faces, and with two they covered their feet, and with two they flew. And one called to another and said:

'Holy, holy, holy is the Lord of hosts; the whole earth is full of his glory.'

The pivots on the thresholds shook at the voices of those who called, and the house filled with smoke. And I said: 'Woe is me! I am lost, for I am a man of unclean lips, and I live among a people of unclean lips; yet my eyes have seen the King, the Lord of hosts!'

Then one of the seraphs flew to me, holding a live coal that had been taken from the altar with a pair of tongs. The seraph touched my mouth with it and said: 'Now that this has touched your lips, your guilt has departed and your sin is blotted out.' Then I heard the voice of the Lord saying, 'Whom shall I send, and who will go for us?' And I said, 'Here am I; send me!'

ες

- Listen again to the verses, read in a different voice.
- Is there a word, or a sentence, that jumps out at you? Which of these words are for you today? Why?
- Either in pairs or in the main group, share with each other the word or phrase that stood out.

Read through once more with a different reader. Has that word or phrase changed?

DISCUSSION TOPICS

Sometimes it can be difficult to start a conversation, especially on a sensitive topic. For the discussion part of the session we have provided a series of conversation starters. We have found the best way to run this part of the session is to photocopy the grid of questions, cut them out, fold and place in a bowl. Encourage group members to take a question, read it out and discuss as a group. The randomness of this can help people to open up more than if the 'leader' asks the questions directly.

Don't feel you have to try and 'answer' all the questions, the main aim is to have a fruitful and interesting discussion. Scan the questions first to see if any might be unhelpful or triggering for people in your group and exclude them. You can also leave the option to people to pass on a question if they wish.

You may wish also to write some discussion questions of your own on this theme that will suit your context. Ideally, this section of the session should feel relaxed and informal.

Jenny seems unprepared. Are we always ready for our calling?

Do Jenny's mixed feelings resonate with something you have experienced?

What effect do you think poverty had, and has, on vocation?

What effect do you think gender had, and has, on vocation?

Can you think of any examples of vocation that inspire you?

How does your church help you to explore or express your vocation?

Have you ever recognised another's vocation? How?

What did you do?

Is a calling fixed, or can it
change over a lifetime?

*'Tell me, what is it you plan to do
with your one wild and precious life?'*
Mary Oliver, 'The Summer Day'

How have *Call the Midwife* and other
people helped you to understand
vocation and calling? Have you a new
or better understanding?

Is vocation something you plan, or
something that happens?

Do you have a calling or vocation you
feel able to share?

RESPONSE TIME

Below are some suggestions for activities to respond to the Bible reading and group discussion. You may wish to use one or a few of these suggestions or come up with an idea of your own. Appropriate music could be played to encourage a prayerful atmosphere. You may wish to begin and end with a time of silence.

1. Create a word-cloud of words you associate with vocation and calling.

2. Make a map or timeline of your life so far and mark the points where you have felt a strong pull or calling to a way of living or being. Share your map or timeline with another person in the group.

3. Make a poster for your church that helps people to recognise and explore what vocation and calling mean.

4. In pairs, take two minutes each to observe and share, without interruption, gifts and qualities you recognise in each other.

5. Write a letter to Jenny, or someone you know, to help them recognise and embrace their vocation.

You may wish to close the response time by singing this chant or another suitable song:

In the Lord I'll be ever thankful;
in the Lord I will rejoice.
Look to God; do not be afraid.
Lift up your voices the Lord is near;
lift up your voices the Lord is near.

(Taizé)

This session may have touched on some difficult, and personal themes.

Invite a time of stillness so that people can think about something that they have found challenging or an action they need to undertake in response to this session.

FINAL PRAYER

Spend some time in silent prayer praying for the person to your right. Then read this prayer in conclusion:

Visit this place, O Lord, we pray,
and drive far from it the snares of the enemy;
may your holy angels dwell with us and guard
    us in peace,
and may your blessing be always upon us;
Through Jesus Christ our Lord.
Amen.

PART 6

LIVING WITH DEATH

THEOLOGICAL
REFLECTION
by the Revd Juliet Stephenson

Juliet was previously the director of the Good Funeral Company and is a priest in the Church of England.

Comfy, cosy, predictable and sanitised. That's what some people say about the wonderful drama series *Call the Midwife*. I suspect these are people who have never watched it! For what this series gives those who invest in the run time of 50 mins per episode, is grit, guts, reality, warts and all. Nothing is hidden or swept under the carpet in this series. From religion and faith, babies born out of wedlock, mixed-race relationships, underage pregnancies, terminations, domestic violence, thalidomide, same-sex relationships, alcoholism, learning difficulties, death, bereavement and heartache. It's all there - and without too much searching.

The stories from Nonnatus House, the Sisters and the midwives and their friends, give to the viewer a taste of life 'back in the day', when things were tough, men were men and women were women. We sometimes cringe at the sight of Dr Turner examining a woman with a cigarette in his mouth, and a woman being shunned because she isn't wearing a wedding ring, but this is reflective of the times, and we go along with it as so we should!

There is no doubt about it that peppered throughout the twelve series (so far) of *Call the Midwife*, we see many births, but we are also subjected to the sadness of death. In the mid-1950s, when the first series was set, the infant mortality rate was approximately 20 births in every 1000. The incidences of stillbirth were similar too. So, death is present in all its sadness; from the babies who we never got chance to meet or name, to the beloved characters who we wept and broke our hearts for as they died. As the episodes progress and we become more familiar with the characters of the story, we are given insight to the life of the religious order of nuns (The Order of St Raymond Nonnatus), and are in the 'cure of souls' of the blessed curate Mr Hereward. It does therefore seem curious that throughout the drama we are rarely in the parish church, or witness an occasional office, of baptism, wedding or funeral service.

This chapter takes on the challenge to seek out only some of the incidences of death in the series, and asks us the question, what does our faith give to us, when we are faced with a death of someone we know? And what value do we place upon a life, dependent upon their age, race, intellect or role in the community?

In the late 1950s in Poplar, we are given our first glimpse of what was a very poor and typical community in the East End of London. As previously mentioned, infant mortality and incidences of still birth were prevalent, and life and death, were a thin veil apart. Coming out of the post war years, the knowledge of love and loss was heavy in the air, and this was meant to be a time for the future: baby boomers, a new world of hope, a future filled with peace. And so, that old 'make do and mend' mentality is seen to be replaced with those who want to better themselves, and give their children what they sadly had lost, or unfortunately never had. We witness the rise of technology, the introduction of 'family planning', high rise blocks of flats and ownership of motorcars.

The earliest example of this 'world made a better place' attitude, is given us through the heart-warming tale of brother and sister Frank and Peggy (Season 1, episode 5). The siblings were left as infants in the workhouse. Tragic circumstances separated them, but eventually as adults they were reunited. Overjoyed, and never wanting to be apart again, they spent each day with one another. A cleaner at Nonnatus House, Peggy was heartbroken when her brother was taken ill. Diagnosed with pancreatic cancer, the prognosis was poor, and following treatment he returned home to be nursed by the religious sisters, nurses and also his beloved sister Peggy. Whilst in their bungalow, nurse Jenny Lee, makes the observation that the brother and sister share a bed, and are living as man and wife. The shock is shared only by the secular nurses, who declare the horror of incest. The religious sisters however, reconcile themselves to the fact attributed to Sister Julienne, that 'theirs was true love that made the two richer.'

Following Frank's death, Peggy simply wants to spend time with him. They wash and prepare his body, as the voice over says: 'A dying person needs to have someone with them – hold their hand – whisper a few words …'

Sister Julienne delays calling the funeral director, to allow them one last night together. This is the opportunity for Peggy to join her beloved brother. Perhaps the final conversation with the sister helped to make her mind up to take just enough of the morphine on the bedside table.

'How do I "be" without him?' asks Peggy. 'Draw strength from knowing that one day you will meet him again', Sister Julienne replies.

For some, the ministry to the dying, is seen to be the ordained minister's role, and yet here, there is no vicar, curate or minister. But only religious sisters and laity. They are adequately prepared, and provide exactly what is needed, without reference to any liturgical books or garments. It is simply a beautiful, incarnational thing to see.

SECRET SUFFERING

In the example of Peggy and Frank, we see love in action. Neither wants the other to be traumatised by the knowledge of what is inevitable, and thinks they are hiding the truth from one another.

Consider:

- Would you want to know you had a terminal illness?
- Would you share details? Keep it private?
- Public sharing via social media is commonplace

for many who are facing treatment and palliative care, what do you think about this?

- The siblings were going to struggle to be alone, how do you reconcile the final actions of Peggy?
- Accompanying the dying ... what does this mean to you?

There are losses of infants in this series, sadly too many to comment upon individually. However, one in particular stands out to me as providing insight into how we approach the death of a longed-for child. In the second episode of Season 2, Cynthia is giving encouragement to Irene Kelly as she delivers her first child. Irene's mother is in the room and playing a fine role as assistant midwife with the hot water and towels. The child is born and wrapped in the very same blanket that her mum Irene was. The proud father is called into the room, and nurse Cynthia places the baby into his strong Irish arms. In a tender moment, the towering man whispers to his new born, 'May you never want for anything', and borrowing a coin, which he swears he will repay when he is back at work, he places the coin into the infant's hand for good luck. The child is surrounded with the love of his little family, and all appears to be well.

Cynthia returns the following day, to a bright and cheerful Irene, who says her baby 'ain't cried once'. On inspection, sadly the baby is not breathing, and against all hope he sadly dies. Help is called, Dr Turner and Sister Julienne arrive, too late.

Here we witness the ministry to the dead, once again, provided by the nun. The baby is named Thomas by the nun and blessed. She recites Scripture, 'I am the resurrection and the life saith the Lord', and he is wrapped up and taken away for a post-mortem examination.

In life, the child has everything he needed, clothing, a home, the love of two parents. In death, he is poor. No money is available for the burial for baby Thomas. It was commonplace in those days to place dead infants inside the coffins of other adults who had died. Nothing speaks of sheer poverty as much as this. Imagine not having a grave marked for your longed-for child.

As the storyline unfolds, we are given this wonderful short dialogue, which speaks of kindness and community. Nurse Miller concerned for the family says, 'They're having to bury baby Thomas in the coffin of a local woman who passed away last night. I can't bear it for them.' Knowing there to be a solution, Sister Julienne replies, 'There is a charitable fund. We can find the details for them and help them with their application.'

Although this is a fine idea, Cynthia Miller has reservations, 'Mr Kelly is far too proud. He'd see it as begging.' And then, the beauty of kindness, comes straight from the heart of Sister Monica Joan and she donates money from her own funds in order that the child has a proper burial.

Thankfully nowadays, we have benefit systems in place to help fund child funerals, and the churches perform services for those up to 18-years-old without fee – but sadly it was not always so.

THE POVERTY OF DEATH

The sorrow of death seems to be even sadder when the hello and goodbye are so close together. The child, unbaptised, dies. The family name him and can't even pay for a burial. In today's society, many die without family or funds for a funeral. Commonly known as 'pauper's funerals', local authorities are obliged to fulfil an obligation as a public health funeral.

Take time to consider:

- The importance of having a name before God.
- What does it mean to mourn for someone you do not know? This could be an unborn infant, a child yet to be named or show its character, the homeless, unknown and those lost to society.
- Talk a little about what you understand 'funeral poverty' to mean.

The curate of the parish Tom Hereward, who is always referred to as 'Mr', is introduced to us in Season 3. We see little evidence of him performing actual liturgical duties, but he becomes one of the central characters in the saddest storyline given to us in Season 8 of the series.

After a failed relationship with Trixie, we find Tom strike up a close friendship with another young midwife, Barbara Gilbert. It is whilst on a mission to South Africa, during the Christmas Special 2016, that this relationship blossoms, and on their return the young couple get engaged. The wedding is conducted by Barbara's father, a clergyman, Nurse Crane is the bridesmaid, and after a short stay in

Birmingham whilst Tom is covering a parish illness, they return to Poplar.

Before leaving Nonnatus House, Sister Julienne assured the newly-married midwife that there would always be a role for her in their team, and Barbara was delighted to be reinstated to the job she was made for, working amongst the people she loved.

Unfortunately, Barbara develops meningitis, and falls seriously ill. The illness of Barbara is central to the other stories during this season of the drama. Her elevation from competent, caring midwife, to wife of the curate, has placed her as a somewhat more vital a character in the community. As well as playing her role as one of the saviours of the antenatal world, she also now has another more spiritual role to perform in her new clerical status.

From her hospital bed, Barbara relishes the dreamy talk of a country parish, a church living where both could fulfil their newfound ministerial role as a clerical couple. Here they would raise their children. Here they would be an example to congregations of what a loving, faithful Christian marriage could look like. Here they would build their future.

For her to have been re-employed to work as a midwife in this intermediate time of the curate's role, was quite remarkable, it seems, for Barbara to still be in the paid role as nurse, gives some weight to the modern outlook of this holy pair. They had a bright future ahead of them, which is why what happens next seems even more desperate.

While Barbara is out of action, we witness the

other midwives covering her rounds, and we see the kindness of patients, who have a great affection for Nurse Hereward. One kind mother gives a gift of an angel ornament, which Barbara cherishes as it watches over her.

On the ward, Barbara is isolated, for risk of infection. Her husband Tom is constantly by her side; in a daze, he walks back to the convent in the rain, soaked through, his face shows despair, and the cruel pain of utter anguish as he frets about the health of his beloved wife. The empathy shown here comes from the older nurse Phyllis. She and Barbara made a special bond while on their mission to South Africa, and the support Tom receives from her during the following days, is the strength that he needs.

When we are sitting, watching and waiting for good news, for a glimmer of light, for someone to turn the corner and begin to recover from illness, it's the quiet solid friendships that are the backbone to our support network. It seems that the focus is on Tom. The community are asking about Barbara's health, and constantly about her husband and how he is coping. Sadly, close friends get bumped down a peg or two. It's the next of kin who we worry about. And yet, we will all have experienced this ourselves; sometimes the nearest and dearest only appear when the chips are down. The steady, grounded, caring, practical and loving friends who are just 'there because' are pushed aside. Their upset goes unnoticed, their tears go un-wiped. Nurse Phyllis Crane, has shared so much with Barbara over the years spent together, she has a real fondness for her, and yet outwardly can't seem to remove the veil of 'nurse' and let her sadness out.

In this episode we have been given insight into the spiritual life of midwife Lucille, who finds a home in a Caribbean house church. She asks Phyllis if she'd like to pray with her for Barbara. Phyllis uncomfortable with the offer, replies kindly, 'Please don't think me ungrateful. Pray all you like for Barbara, but don't ask me to do it. I'll just do what I'm doing, quietly.' This community is together in its sadness, and together in its willing for a miracle, it's just that this community does things differently!

A corner is turned, all looks like it's going to be well. Nurse Crane draws up a visitor's rota, so all the community members can come and visit Barbara; she catches up on news, she smiles, listens and seems to be on the mend. But a glance at her fingertips, and a quiet medical consultation with her best friend Phyllis, sees Barbara all too aware that the septicaemia is worsening, and her end is imminent. It's a tender, if dreadfully sad discourse between the two soul mates. As nurses, they both know what this means. This, we could not have witnessed between cleric husband and wife.

And so, begins the end. Reverend Tom recites the Twenty-third Psalm, Phyllis is at his side, and both are holding Barbara's hands as she slips away.

As the community is given the news, we see a wave of disbelief, grief, despair and utter sadness come upon the friends. This was not expected. This was not fair. This will shake their faith. This might break them entirely. And yet, as the funeral scenes unfold, the church is filled with faces of those who loved this brilliant, charming and dedicated young midwife, all there to pay their last respects.

The bridesmaid-turned-eulogiser, stands in place beside the coffin and reads the words of a poem. She looks up and encourages a mother of a crying child to let it be. 'None of us objects to the sound of a crying child.' The service continues, whilst the grief-stricken husband stares in disbelief. A service that he has performed on many occasions, is now being done for his beautiful young wife, and it's all too surreal.

The wake follows, Phyllis disappears to be alone, and the eeriness settles upon them all. But the business of life marches on for Nonnatus House even in the face of death, and a needy labouring woman beckons. Tom grieves. He reflects upon the bereavement advice he has handed out countless times to others in his situation. And in a bid to move on, he plans his future on a mission in New Guinea without his wife beside him.

The episode ends as a baby is born, a child destined for adoption, but allowed enough time with its mother to be given the gift of a name. 'It popped into my head, just before, I don't know why. Barbara. Must have been floating round the room like a moth or a butterfly or something. Waiting to be caught.'

GRIEVING AS A PROFESSIONAL

'To everything there is a season, and a time to every purpose under the heaven: a time to be born, and a time to die.' Ecclesiastes 3: 1-2a (KJV)

147

The significant death of Barbara, one of the main characters, gives us a series of things to consider:

- Should it make a difference when an 'upstanding member of the community' dies?
- Barbara's illness and demise were well followed; how hard must it be to grieve when all eyes are upon you?
- How do close friends grieve, in the shadow of a chief mourner?
- Consider helpful bereavement advice? How do professionals cope with a close death? (Think about medics, clerics, funeral operatives.)
- What is the place of prayer in this episode? Is an offer to 'pray with you' uncomfortable or helpful? To what extent do people of faith just go into 'autopilot' mode?
- In the face of death, how is our faith tested?

COURSE MATERIALS

by the Revd Bryony Taylor

OPENING PRAYER

A candle is lit and these words are said:

'This candle is to remind us of God's presence with us.'

Silence is kept.

OPTIONAL: WATCH CALL THE MIDWIFE
Watch Series 1, episode 5 from 30.23-31.00: Sister Julienne comforts someone who's lost a loved one

INTRODUCTION

Group leaders may wish to read this out loud or introduce the theme in their own words.

Throughout all the series of *Call the Midwife*, life is punctuated not only by birth but also death. As we watch this programme set 50 years in the past we are reminded of how we have pushed the acknowledgement of death and dying to the very sidelines of our society. Death is the final taboo; it is more clinical now and very few of us have seen a dead body. In the time of *Call the Midwife*, it was still common for people to die at home and for people to gather to 'lay out' the body. What hasn't changed, however, is that we still all experience death, bereavement and sadness in many forms – it is just not spoken about very much. The many sad scenes of death in *Call the Midwife* help us to explore what we feel about death, and at one step removed, help us to reflect on our own experiences. At the centre of the Christian faith is our belief in the resurrection and yet we rarely talk about death and bereavement. This session is an opportunity to speak about this taboo subject but very much in the context of our belief in the resurrection.

LECTIO DIVINA

Listen carefully as someone reads this passage from the Bible, then take some time afterwards to reflect in silence on what you have just heard.

The passage is provided in two translations here, you may wish to use a different version (visit Biblegateway.com to find alternative versions). Sometimes it is helpful to provide group members with a copy so that they can read along.

1 CORINTHIANS 15:35-44 NEW REVISED STANDARD VERSION

But someone will ask, 'How are the dead raised? With what kind of body do they come?' Fool! What you sow does not come to life unless it dies. And as for what you sow, you do not sow the body that is to be, but a bare seed, perhaps of wheat or of some other grain. But God gives it a body as he has chosen, and to each kind of seed its own body. Not all flesh is alike, but there is one flesh for human beings, another for animals, another for birds, and another for fish. There are both heavenly bodies and earthly bodies, but the glory of the heavenly is one thing, and that of the earthly is another. There is one glory of the sun, and another glory of the moon, and another glory of the stars; indeed, star differs from star in glory.

So, it is with the resurrection of the dead. What is sown is perishable, what is raised is imperishable. It is sown in dishonour, it is raised in glory. It is sown in weakness; it is raised in power. It is sown a physical body; it is raised a spiritual body. If there is a physical body, there is also a spiritual body.

1 CORINTHIANS 15:35-44 THE MESSAGE (MSG)

Some sceptic is sure to ask, 'Show me how resurrection works. Give me a diagram; draw me a picture. What does this "resurrection body" look like?' If you look at this question closely, you realize how absurd it is. There are no diagrams for this kind of thing. We do have a parallel experience in gardening. You plant a 'dead' seed; soon there is a flourishing plant. There is no visual likeness between seed and plant. You could never guess what a tomato would look like by looking at a tomato seed. What we plant in the soil and what grows out of it don't look anything alike. The dead body that we bury in the ground and the resurrection body that comes from it will be dramatically different.

You will notice that the variety of bodies is

stunning. Just as there are different kinds of seeds, there are different kinds of bodies—humans, animals, birds, fish—each unprecedented in its form. You get a hint at the diversity of resurrection glory by looking at the diversity of bodies not only on earth but in the skies—sun, moon, stars—all these varieties of beauty and brightness. And we're only looking at pre-resurrection "seeds"—who can imagine what the resurrection "plants" will be like!

This image of planting a dead seed and raising a live plant is a mere sketch at best, but perhaps it will help in approaching the mystery of the resurrection body—but only if you keep in mind that when we're raised, we're raised for *good*, alive forever! The corpse that's planted is no beauty, but when it's raised, it's glorious. Put in the ground weak, it comes up powerful. The seed sown is natural; the seed grown is supernatural—same seed, same body, but what a difference from when it goes down in physical mortality to when it is raised up in spiritual immortality!

ശ

- Listen again to the verses, read in a different voice.
- Is there a word, or a sentence, that jumps out at you? Which of these words are for you today? Why?
- Either in pairs or in the main group, share with each other the word or phrase that stood out.

Read through once more with a different reader. Has that word or phrase changed?

DISCUSSION TOPICS

Sometimes it can be difficult to start a conversation, especially on a sensitive topic. For the discussion part of the session we have provided a series of conversation starters. We have found the best way to run this part of the session is to photocopy the grid of questions, cut them out, fold and place in a bowl. Encourage group members to take a question, read it out and discuss as a group. The randomness of this can help people to open up more than if the 'leader' asks the questions directly.

Don't feel you have to try and 'answer' all the questions, the main aim is to have a fruitful and interesting discussion. Scan the questions first to see if any might be unhelpful or triggering for people in your group and exclude them. You can also leave the option to people to pass on a question if they wish.

You may wish also to write some discussion questions of your own on this theme that will suit your context. Ideally, this section of the session should feel relaxed and informal.

Accompanying the dying ... what does this mean to you?

What kind of things would you like to happen at your funeral?

How do you feel about being asked to wear bright colours to a funeral?

What is the difference between a celebration of life and a funeral?

Who is a funeral for – the dead person or their friends and family?

What does it mean to mourn for someone you do not know?

What are the similarities between birth and death?

Do dying people need a midwife too?

What does resurrection mean to you?

What are helpful things to say to a bereaved person?

What are unhelpful things to say to a bereaved person?

RESPONSE TIME

Below are some suggestions for activities to respond to the Bible reading and group discussion. You may wish to use one or a few of these suggestions or come up with an idea of your own. Appropriate music could be played to encourage a prayerful atmosphere. You may wish to begin and end with a time of silence.

1. Spend some time talking about a loved one who has died, what you loved about them, maybe tell a funny story. Then light a candle for them.
2. Think through and write down what hymns, music and readings you would like at your own funeral.
3. Take some seed paper and write the names of loved ones who have died on the paper in a time of prayer. Take the paper home and water it and see what grows from it.
4. Share with one another any Bible verses or poems that have helped you when you've been bereaved or that you have heard at a funeral yourself.
5. Play some music and while the music is playing encourage people to take a pebble from a bowl and place it on the floor – together create a cross shape from your pebbles. The pebbles can represent lost loved ones or other bereavements.

You may wish to close the response time by singing this chant or another suitable song:

The Lord is my light, my light and salvation,
in God I trust, in God I trust.

(Taizé)

This session may have touched on some difficult, and personal themes.

Invite a time of stillness so that people can think about something that they have found challenging or an action they need to undertake in response to this session.

FINAL PRAYER

Spend some time in silent prayer praying for the person to your right. Then read this prayer in conclusion:

Visit this place, O Lord, we pray,
and drive far from it the snares of the enemy;
may your holy angels dwell with us and guard
    us in peace,
and may your blessing be always upon us;
through Jesus Christ our Lord.
Amen.

THE ALL OF LIFE COURSE IS DESIGNED AND EDITED BY:

The Revd Bryony Taylor is a telly addict and Anglican priest based in Derbyshire. She is passionate about making real life connect with faith.

Fr David Twomey, an Anglican priest and airport chaplain, who enjoys a wide variety of television and film. His other passions in life are beer, border collies and the Book of Common Prayer (though not necessarily in that order).

The Revd Rebecca Amoroso, an Anglican priest, university chaplain, tutor and former prison chaplain. She is passionate about equality, inclusivity and justice.